Survive the Modern World

How *to be* ONLINE & also be HAPPY

Issy Beech

Hardie Grant
BOOKS

Introduction

They made it sound so sinless, didn't they? 'Surfing the internet'.

They should have called it 'cage-fighting the internet' or 'riding the internet like it's a malfunctioning mechanical bull'. Or 'wading through piles of garbage and occasionally, *maybe*, doing a small laugh inside your head'.

'Surfing the internet' sounds very chill and cool, actually, and not at all like being online is. But fair's fair(ish), the early surfers of the internet weren't to know about all ... *this*. How could they? Going online back in 1994 *was* kind of akin to a nice spot of surfing – just a few hundred thousand people at any one time, bouncing around, dipping in and out of a hundred chat rooms and watching as the first virtual libraries went live. Before the reality-shifting advent of content farms and Cambridge Analytica and Facetune. Back when the possibilities felt endless and full of glistening potential, instead of twisted and unfair and maddening and, you know, planet-destroying. So, not *totally* unbeach-like.

Twenty-something years later, going online is more like – forgive me – being dunked, over and over, all day. And then crawling onto shore with your swimsuit around your knees. And then trying to laugh about it. And then getting heatstroke in the car on the way home.

Whether you're holding this book because you bought it or because you're in somebody's house and you weren't sure what to do with your hands: welcome. Thanks for meeting me here. I know how busy you've been.

We don't really know each other but you clearly belong here, because this book is for people who spend a lot of time online, and that's just about everybody. More particularly, these pages are a place for those of us who aren't sure if being online even feels that good anymore, and that's obviously you because why else would you pick up something called *How to Be Online and Also Be Happy?*

If you're anything like me, it's very likely that you spend a whole lot of time on your phone, tablet or computer – possibly all of your waking hours – looking at apps and websites. And maybe you sometimes feel like that should change, but most of the time you'd prefer not to think about it. Because everybody does it, because it's normal, because it feels nice, because it helps. But it's getting harder to ignore.

You may have spent the last few years feeling an uncomfortable medley of vaguely interested in, extremely shocked and deeply hurt by the internet. You may have spent many nights – and mornings and mid-mornings and afternoons – staring listlessly at screens of all shapes and sizes, mouth agape, thinking, 'Wait. We're *allowed* to do that?'.

When did it all get so ... the way it is? With the news and trends and challenges and paid partnerships and all the *people, saying* stuff. How did something we all adored and desperately needed become so hellish? Is it the endless avalanche of information? Or the overwhelming size of it all? The monetisation? Data mining? The millions of voices? The doxxing, the catfishing? The yelling? The velocity? The brands that tweet? The couples that prank each other?

A study conducted in 2019 found that positive experiences on social media didn't necessarily make users feel any happier, but negative online experiences did amplify feelings of sadness. Because we're hardwired with what psychologists call a negativity bias – our tendency to feel, remember and fixate on negative stimuli more than positive ones – we're likely to take with us the bad online moments, and forget the good ones more easily. Which means that even if the time we spend online and looking at screens is equal parts fulfilling and disturbing, we're probably still walking away feeling more crappy than good.

It's ok. We're here and we're together, and we're going to try to make it all a little more bearable. First things first: stop punishing yourself for being addicted to one of the coolest things on Earth. It's not your fault. It can be so good on there and abstaining from going online is not for everybody. Especially when you're one of the many people chained to an internet connection for a job. What I do think is possible, even necessary, is rethinking how we use it.

Most days, my internet use consists of emailing, writing and researching for work – fine - peppered heavily by checking my personal emails over and over for no reason, scrolling Twitter in three-minute blocks, for no reason, unlocking my phone, looking at stories and, eventually, inevitably, ending up in some deep, dark corner of a stranger's Instagram comments and developing a heated opinion about a conversation that is none of my business that occurred twelve hours ago. Not so fine.

When are we actually *using* the internet – searching, registering, thinking, feeling – and when are we just tumbling into the void, staring at the screen, going agreeably numb? Do we follow accounts on social media because they make us feel good, or because we're addicted to not missing out? Are we spending time online in places that challenge us and help us grow, or are we building little echo chambers? Are we using our platforms to seek approval? Are we playing into the hands of the monoliths like Facebook and Twitter? Are we connecting, or are our worlds shrinking? When are we validating and promoting content that has adverse affects on others, and when are we contributing in a way that feels good and kind and thoughtful? Do we engage with the content that moves us, or are we too used to just consuming and walking away? And are we spoiled in thinking that we deserve the internet, a place where content is free and repercussions, for the most part, don't exist?

A clinical psychologist once told me that changing our behaviour over time ultimately changes us as people. If we make certain changes in our lives – like picking up our phones less often, following more rewarding accounts, or adding positive noise to the internet – and repeat them, we are very likely to become those changes. To me, this means if we're unhappy with our onlineness, the little changes each of us make in our day-to-day shouldn't just change the way we feel; they should theoretically change who we are.

In the coming chapters, you'll find ideas and practical approaches for spending your time online more thoughtfully. Your feeds should be a place of delight and nourishment, but equally important is that your time offline doesn't just feel like moments between staring at screens.

 # ACTIVITY

Just how online are you?

For one day, make a record of:

* The number of minutes you spend looking at a device while in bed

* The number of times you look at your phone or tablet screen without prompting

* The number of times you reach for your phone or tablet while in the middle of another task

* The number of times you're online and you forget what you were doing

* At the end of the day, tally your score.

10-50: You're fine, and you should probably re-gift (or put back) this book.

51-100: You're average, normal, if you will. While it might be time to change some things, you're not in any grave danger. Proceed if you wish.

101 and above: You're in dire straits, baby. But so is most of the world. You know what you need to do.

Chapter One

WHAT *Even* Happened, Though?

The first website I remember visiting was a website that I made. Except I didn't make it, my friend Nabila did because I had no idea how and she was a lot smarter than me. Mostly, I just sat there behind her in the half-dark of her parents' study, helping her choose between colours and sparkles and telling her which images I thought should be put where. Our website – my first website but not Nabila's – was a fan site dedicated to the movie *Titanic*. Which is perfectly normal because the year was 1998 and this was the most important thing on the planet at the time. And my god, it was *wonderful*. Orange and glittering with animated bits and pictures of Kate Winslet with ornate frames that danced from side to side. It wasn't just a site or a page: it was a *place*. A place I couldn't stop thinking about, not in the car on the way home, not during dinner and not later, in bed, where I lay staring at the ceiling, completely electrified.

Before apps came along, these websites were the internet. Chat rooms and fan sites and pages dedicated to extremely specific eras in history, laid out in impossible-to-read royal blue Times New Roman.

From *Titanic* fan sites we, as a collective, moved onto stranger (and better) things. Rotten.com and Neopets and Blingee. Message boards, which were really just chat rooms with more rules. Angelfire and DeviantArt and Fandomination.net. We were chatting to our friends and randoms on MSN Messenger, changing our statuses twice daily to read extremely important things like .::**can i borrow a kiss? i promise i'll give it back**::.. From there, it escalated thrillingly into MySpace and its skins and top friends, teaching ourselves HTML, video editing and Photoshop. Quickly becoming expert at finding our crushes' homes on Google Street

View, selling our things on eBay when we needed money for eBay purchases, and telling all of Facebook we were *not feeling great but doubt anybody actually cares*. Then we were tweeting and posting to Instagram, and emailing ten hours a day for a job. And before we knew it, everything had moved online. And then some.

Banking, shopping, meeting new people and falling in love went online. And in no time we were doing dances, doing other dances, and dropping buckets of ice water on our heads for charity. Waking up to like, dislike, share, share, share. Scrolling into the Great Beyond.

It's easy to look back on it all and wonder what happened, to ask if our desire for making the internet Do Everything was part of the human condition and inevitable or if we could have slowed the momentum back when we still had time.

 # EXPLAINER

A mini timeline of it all

1966
ARPANET, the data-sharing network that laid the foundations
for the internet, is switched on

1978
Gary Thuerk sends the world's first spam email

1991
The web becomes worldwide

1993
Marc Andreessen, a student at Illinois University, develops
the first web browser Mosaic

1994
The first pizza is ordered using the internet

1996
The first pop-up ad is served

1997
The internet goes wireless with the introduction of WiFi

1999
Napster makes music free

2000
43 per cent of internet users say they would miss going online 'a lot'

2001
The world meets Friendster, the first ever social media platform

2003
The Pirate Bay begins facilitating peer-to-peer file sharing online

2005
Me at the zoo is the first video on YouTube,
posted by co-founder Jawed Karim

2006
'LOOK HOT In 5 Minutes or Less ...' is the first makeup
tutorial uploaded to YouTube

2008
@dril posts his first tweet

2011
Spotify brings legal music streaming to the world

2014
Serial from This American Life leads the podcast boom

2016
Facebook admits to inflating viewership metrics
by as much as 900 per cent

2018
Kids and teens film themselves eating TidePods in the
hopes of going viral

2020
A young man who licked a toilet seat in the 'coronavirus challenge'
is hospitalised after testing positive for the virus

When did the internet start making us sad?

It can't have been before or during 2002, when we were still skipping home from work or school two steps at a time in the dizzying anticipation of logging onto message boards to weigh in on discussions about our favourite bands and our favourite bands' favourite bands, with other internet users in Jakarta and San Francisco. And it wasn't in 2006, when we were personalising our MySpaces and blogs into the grey hours of the early morning – a time in history so supremely nice that I often look back and envy us. Maybe it was in 2012 and 2013, when Facebook and Twitter became public companies, owned by shareholders.

Or maybe it really all began to suck somewhere around 2016, when an American election was undermined using Facebook and our precious viral videos – one of the internet's greatest gifts – were finally and wholly co-opted by marketers and influencers, and used to sell us more stuff we don't need or want. Around the time that many of us fully accepted – arms open, eyes closed – equating our self-worth with the amount of likes and comments and all-round attention we received on social media. Around the time that the internet stopped being about us, the average household user, and crossed over to become a fully-fledged business, our attention and time was the currency. And also the product. Now, when we open our favourite apps, we're not likely to blink at the one ad for every five posts, or that every key we press will result in some kind of clumsily targeted content. It's unusual to go more than a few seconds without seeing an altered body in an image or video, or to casually witness an interaction that tears apart the very fabric of your reality. It's not unusual to be told by a chip company that Black Lives Matter, or to be emailed about the best new Netflix shows by a bed linen company.

To watch a TikTok star wink at their iPhone camera while giving money to someone in need, or to learn of somebody's death from a pile-on Twitter joke.

Peter Dodds and Chris Danforth from the University of Vermont developed the Hedonometer – a live graph that gauges online happiness by tracking the positive and negative words used on Twitter each day. Since late 2015, the Hedonometer has been veering steadily downward. Meaning, the internet and what we're bearing witness to on there doesn't just feel more miserable and hopeless than before, it actually kind of is.

Maybe if we logged on once or twice a day, we wouldn't feel so smothered by all the content. But our online-ness is now practically constant.

Do we miss missing the internet?

When did the internet stop being something to *go* on and start being something we never left? Probably around the time we annihilated the idea of 'online now'. When we did away with the green 'I'm online' dot, what we were saying was 'Am I here? Am I not? Go on, just try me'. With direct messages and push notifications, we were invited to be constantly and instantly contactable. I message you, you immediately respond – or, at the very least, immediately screen my message. Maybe it really was meant to make us more efficient but what it's doing, more and more, is making us unable to concentrate and impossible to surprise. Our attention is splintered, our connections feel shallower and our retention is weak. Having access to anything you want any time of day is, surprisingly, not a dream. It's actually a bit of a nightmare.

If you were born after the turn of the millennium, you should know it wasn't always this way. There used to be a palpable thrill, logging onto an app or browser: the suspense, the ding of entering the chat, the green dot. It was so electric because it wasn't immediate, or constant. Back in the early aughts, when my family got our first computer, there wasn't just logging on: there were various *stages* of logging on. Our computer was a big, black, buzzing IBM, one we only 'booted up' between school and dinner, then again between dinner and bedtime, taking turns on it for half hours so our eyes didn't go square.

Turning it on meant pressing a button and waiting. Then there was logging in and waiting. And going online meant dialling up and waiting, searching things and waiting, and logging into instant messenger apps and waiting. And though this process took approximately sixty years each time, it actually seemed faster than the speed of light, because prior to this, the internet had been nowhere, at least not in people's homes. We got news from the TV, the radio and print media, there were no notifications unless you count the answering machine or, of course, from the urchins on street corners in little tweed caps shouting 'Extra! Extra!' and 'Commissioner says no motive for bank heist!'. The internet was somewhere else. Until it wasn't.

How it is now

If you're an average person, you probably touch your phone in the first five minutes after waking. And if you're an actual average person and not one of the people lying on those surveys, you probably touch it immediately. You probably think of it before your eyes are even open. It's likely the source of that incessant noise, after all. And in no time, it's there, shining its blue-ish light on your poor, scrunched up, just-trying-to-get-it-together face. You're feeling that familiar urge to open your favourite app, to start scrolling and catching up. So you do it, because why not?

You tumble into the depths of the infinite scroll. This tweet, that meme, this post, that story. Hardly any of it sticks but it feels good, like staring into space until you go cross-eyed. You don't have to think, not if you don't want to. Not about what day it is or anything else, really. Once you have your phone in hand, you can trust it with all the particulars. So instead of thinking or planning or even feeling, you spend the first moments of your day stupefied.

Most mornings, you probably scroll while somebody you live with showers and gets dressed, and you continue scrolling for however long it takes you to realise that time is, despite appearances, passing and there are things to do. So you shower and you inexplicably take your phone into the bathroom, even though it just sits there on the sink getting a bit damp and then, as you're drying yourself off, you shout questions about the weather and the time at Siri or Ask Google or whoever.

At the kitchen bench, you probably scroll through TikToks and Instagram stories like a maniac; tap tap tap hold tap tap hold tap tap. At some point, you get out the door and play something in your headphones because it's what you do.

On the way into work or school, you're sitting and scrolling or standing and scrolling, jumping between apps and following content into rooms and threads and linkouts until you don't know where you are or how you got there or who's prime minister. Unless it's one of your Off Days, in which case you're listening to a Serious Podcast and only just resisting the itch to pull your phone from your pocket because you're Looking After Your Mental Health.

Either way, by the time you've arrived where you need to be, you know everything. News, memes, jokes, updates, and anything anybody anywhere did while you were asleep. And it doesn't feel good or bad or anything, really. It just is.

Throughout the day, if you don't drive a bus or do kitchen prep or cave dive, you probably pick up your phone again and again ... and again. Sometimes for a reason, but mostly just because you can. Sometimes you're not even picking it up; you're just touching it.

You listen to a PODCAST, while scanning an *ARTICLE*, replying to a TEXT, looking up an ACTOR, and taking an ironic SELFIE *

Flirting with the unlock button and feeling the grooves. Other times, you're not even touching it, you're only looking at it, or even just thinking of it.

I love my little phone. The little kingdom inside it, that I rule over, mercilessly, most of the time. I love all my loyal subjects (emojis) and my trusty steed (Google Maps).

You likely read the internet on the way home too, like most of the people sitting beside you on public transport or in traffic. You listen to a podcast while scanning an article, replying to a text, looking up an actor, and taking an ironic selfie. Doing so many things at once that it somehow becomes more like doing nothing. But you like it because time passes quicker this way, and without feelings for the most part, which can be a relief at the end of the day.

In the evenings, while watching a movie or TV, you probably scroll some more, still unsatiated. By this time of day, you're mostly looking at posts you've already seen, now being reposted by more and more people, being shared in the hundreds of thousands. You'll read ten words into a meme or a tweet or a post before you even realise you've read it before, ten minutes ago as well as ten hours ago, but you'll probably finish reading it anyway. At this point it becomes a game: Find Something I Haven't Seen Yet. Keep mining through the apps until you see something new. And if you can't? There's always bedtime.

In bed, you continue this bizarre ritual, scrolling and tapping through Twitter and Instagram and Snapchat and TikTok in search of *something, anything*. Some new joke or photo, some new thing you can relate to or send to six different friends and three group chats. And when your eyes get heavy and your phone is slipping from your exhausted little hand, you pop it there on the bedside table, centimetres away from your head, and reluctantly turn out the light.

Chapter Two

WHY Do We Do It?

Living huge chunks of our lives online can, and often does, feel genuinely awful. So then why do we keep doing it? The truth is that it's not really the internet's fault, is it? Sure, it can be extremely bad, but it's got beauty and purity in spades. For every Cambridge Analytica, there's a Black Girl Magic and for every Logan Paul there's a Jaboukie Young-White tweet that absolutely decimates him. And just as the internet exhaustively proliferates fake news and extreme body dysmorphia, research actually suggests that the only generation to have grown up wholly online – gen Z – are measurably better for it: more politically active, more socially and environmentally conscious and more likely to prioritise people over profit. Being online is painful, yes, but it also appears to be making us better (though apparently a little miserable). And, while we've cultivated an unbreakable-feeling bond with the internet and the apps – this place of relief where we can feel powerful, informed, hopeful and known – studies show that it's also just having a phone that pleases us. Shiri Melumad and Robert Meyer of the Wharton School at the University of Pennsylvania found that one factor in disclosing ourselves so freely online was that we see our phones as a 'safe space', something we've cultivated a relationship with, something curated, personalised and private. Something that's all ours: shiny, customised, a place of intimacy and safety that's always within reach.

But it's not just addictive, personal and infinite, and there's more to it than just algorithms and good design. The very real truth is that the internet can be absolutely top of the class for connection and belonging. At times, even better than – dare I say it – the real world. No matter how ugly it gets, we're won over again and again by something. Something impossibly stupid or impossibly human; a painfully specific universal truth or joy or bit of nonsense that touches on something in each of us. We rally around these glimmers of light for warmth, our backs to the rest of it for a second, because we need that hope. Because people can be really good. It's a place of belonging for those of us who have felt deprived of belonging. It's a place of self-expression and bravery where we might usually shy away. A silly little song, a glitched-out picture of SpongeBob, a life-affirming article, a perfectly-crafted tweet, six Hairdresser Reacts YouTube videos in a row. The way the forums help define you and the tutorials help you grow. The way one sweet meme can make us feel Alive Together instead of Alive Alone, and the way one beautiful internet friendship can change the course of your life.

There's no pretending that what's on the internet isn't worth a whole lot of our time. In fact, it's enough to make you want to cry with joy.

The internet is especially great when it's funny and honest. The jokes and stories on the internet are out of this world, better than any bookshop or streaming service or cable network if only because, on the internet, *anyone* can find an audience and a voice. You don't have to be rich enough to try, and you don't have to be privileged enough to be given the mic. You can be anyone and your story can be *anything*. Your neighbour, a little kid, a secret genius, some person in their parents' basement, your cool teacher, a loveable mother of five, a great home cook, a stunt person. Jay Versace, Chris Crocker, Gavin, Tabitha Brown, Lou Ratchett, Dril, Paloma Elsesser, Boo the dog, Lauren Servideo, Behrouz Boochani, Timmy Thick, Miumiu Guitargirl, Alok Vaid-Menon, Joanne the Scammer, Lil Miquela. Anyone.

The internet is also good because we need it to live. For the most part, anyway. Using the internet in all its forms is a part of being accepted for the vast majority of people. Being normal, being informed and being thought of. Being online is having a life that doesn't feel lonely or exclusionary because people are reminded you exist. It's being *part of things*. It also means being streamlined, cooperative, accessible and acceptable. Without it, we'd be left behind, because we need it to do all manner of things that make our lives functional. We need it to get paid, to buy stuff, to learn things, to progress. To apply for uni, to rent a car, to be on income support, to pay a bill.

And, of course, we need it to do a whole lot of the stuff that makes us happy in the smallest and most mundane ways, because we've gotten used to it. And to have that taken away might feel, well, terrible. We need it to keep in touch with old friends and people far away. To find out how to shuck an oyster or clean our specific brand of vacuum. To be in the group chat, ask for help, google our symptoms, get directions, buy tickets to stuff, share files, find out when people we like release new music. To find a recipe we can't figure out, or a name we can't remember.

The internet is also good for something very specific and wonderful: the thousands of little paper trails of our many relationships and interactions. An automatic account of the communications between you and another person that you can look back through if you've lost them or miss them, or if you're bored or a little bit tipsy, and you can remember just how lucky and loved you are.

Escaping through the internet

The internet, at its best, is a place of comfort. Like a loving relationship, it's there for you and full of advice. You learn from it, confide in it, find comfort in it, masturbate to it. You teach it to know you and very often it teaches itself, which is generally fine but then at other times, despicable and terrifying. The internet is also a place of solace because – let's just say it – the real world is often awful. Like many unhealthy habits, using the internet is a nice distraction from other stuff. We don't destructively eat, drink, gamble or exercise just because it feels good; we do it because life is hard and sometimes, we want to turn that off.

Using your phone in the middle of a workday for a solid half an hour without blinking sometimes feels truly good. That beautiful, untouchable feeling of taking all that Real World rubbish, putting it in a little boat and pushing it out to sea. Being occupied instead by things that don't demand your attention at all, but sit there for your amusement.

Not to be underestimated is the internet's ability to be a place of complete non-participation in a world where we constantly feel compelled to do things. This bill, that text, this meeting, that smile from a stranger. You've got to exercise, make money, stay clean, stay healthy, keep going, be vulnerable, be strong, explain yourself, not let things get to you, work hard, be self-deprecating, stay informed, stay positive. You've got to go out into the world every day and interact with people who don't understand or like you, or don't treat you with respect or kindness. You have to exist under systems that exploit you and you have to be brave and say things you're afraid of saying, and work hard and take care of your loved ones, and sometimes put up with them and other times be thankful that they put up with you.

When things are too much on Earth offline, online can feel like the one place where we're not expected to be anything we don't want to be.

Life can be a nightmare. That's not to say there aren't reasons to enjoy living or be in love with your life, but nobody could blame you for being, now and then, absolutely and completely trampled by The Current State of Things.

And the big one? The planet is dying. The planet! The one we live on! It's dying! Each day, we wake up and are expected to pour cereal, answer emails, pay bills, and shower knowing that the planet we live on is dying. Meanwhile, the algorithms are racist.

The phone company owns your nudes. And when The Washington Post asked readers to describe 2020 in one word or phrase, the top three responses were 'lost', 'chaotic' and 'exhausting'.

That's not even taking into account your personal problems, whatever they may be. You might be struggling to pay rent, going through a break-up, grappling with your identity, trying to survive an illness, or you might just be waking up, each and every day, struggling to pinpoint exactly what it is about being human that confounds and troubles you so, but trudging along each minute anyway because as a speck on a slightly larger speck in infinite darkness, there's not much else you can do.

It's no wonder we're addicted to switching off. Whether it's with beauty tutorials, YouTube tarot readings, Buzzfeed quizzes, Twitch streams – whatever. It's better than thinking about how impossibly stacked against us the world feels and how hard we have to fight to fix it.

Are we really switching off by going online?

While we might sometimes tell ourselves we're going online for a simple morsel of respite, the truth is that we're not often given the luxury. Between the conspiracy, surveillance and the endless stream of everyday people trying to go viral, little moments of joy can feel hard to come by on the net. The internet is also where, for the most part, we learn about the world's ills and where we express our rage about them. Yes, it's very often where we go to find communities that care about what we care about, where we mobilise, strategise and agonise, but when we unlock our phones each morning to see the same, tired nonsense, all the rancor and rallying can begin to feel like hurling pebbles at a giant brick wall.

* How do we OFFSET the pain of being online? CREATE MORE GOOD

Here is one solution to your impossible-to-stop doom-scrolling: designate a favourite website or kind of browsing. What do you like best about using the net outside of, like, looking through TikTok? Is it long reads? Clean With Me? Gardening advice? Facebook groups? Thrift hauls? Newsletters? Shopping on Etsy?

Where does your internet use stop being browsing for the sake of it and start being an extension of your wants and needs? Your individuality? Who you are?

When you start defining what it is you like and love about the internet, the desire to stop scrolling for no reason might actually begin to hit you. Instead of letting the infinite wash over you like normal, you might think, 'Wait. Wouldn't I rather be ...'

I like reading columns; advice columns, design columns and columns about relationships. I like reading profiles of people, usually really long ones that take up lots of time about hugely famous people – yes, even when they're not that good. I like watching *Vogue's Beauty Secrets*, especially the ones featuring people with bags under their eyes and cool hair and quirky eye makeup. I like watching old *Bon Appetit* Test Kitchen videos, and most other kinds of cooking videos. I like to watch videos about how they illustrate Ghibli movies, and Oprah segments from the 1990s and 2000s about kids who can see the future, or suburban mums who sustained a head injury and instantly learnt a new language. I like videos that explain how underwater tunnels are built, or how bridges are built, or how anything big and metal or concrete is built. I like to ask Google stupid questions like 'am I sick?' or 'what is wrong with me?', and I love to slide into Wikipedia holes, following hyperlink after hyperlink until I simply can't stand it anymore. I listen to podcasts on Spotify, like *Seek Treatment with Cat and Pat* and *The Read* and Esther Perel-related things, so that my eyes get a break and I feel like I'm socialising.

I like FaceTiming my friends and my family so I feel like I'm keeping in touch, which is what this thing was meant to

ACTIVITY

Define your internet

Being online doesn't just have to be clicking on stuff the feed serves to you. It can, and sometimes should, be more purposeful. Start by defining Your Internet; the kinds of browsing, watching, and reading that feels good to you. Once you know and can name what you like about the internet, it might become more obvious when you're using it in a way that doesn't serve you.

* When do you feel happiest online?

* What are your favourite apps and sites? What do you love about them? Which parts are less good?

* What are your favourite apps and sites? What do you love about them? Which parts are less good?

* What internet stuff makes you feel good and what does it do for you as a person? How does that affect the people in your life?

* When does going online make you feel smarter? Nicer? More understanding? Better to spend time with?

* Which parts of the internet are helping you grow and be happy? And how often do you actually tap into that?

be for, wasn't it? And my favourite thing I have ever found on the internet is a YouTube account by a user with Dissociative Identity Disorder (DID) who posts videos about their life and their identities. I watch everything they post with a twinkle in my eye (probably); videos where they introduce their alters, or build the alters and their 'inner world' using *The Sims*. Videos where they do AMAs about their likes, dislikes and how DID works. This kind of internet is the kind of internet I think I was most enamoured by all those years ago: one that explains the world to you, takes you out of yourself and makes you more thoughtful, all while giving a person a voice.

✳ This cycle of JUDGING and being JUDGED is a black hole in which time disappears, in which I and the people I encounter are all FROZEN in our profiles

Tavi Gevinson

Chapter Three

WHAT *is it* Doing TO US?

We're remembering less

Our attention spans are worse

Our self-esteem is taking a hit

We're actually getting injured

The way we engage with apps and social media, the wider internet, and the devices in our lives, is having a real-world negative effect on our bodies and minds.

Being online is as painful as it is joyful because we're contorting our bodies, we're boring ourselves, we're losing brain power, we're haemorrhaging empathy and we're witnessing the micro-horrors that live in our world – and we're expected not to flinch.

Because there are memes, feeds and shiny little distractions, it's easy to forget about this stuff. The anger, the obscenity, the greed and the shamelessness. And while there's enough good online to keep us happy, all that other stuff is still going somewhere.

In any one day, a person with a social media account is extremely likely to read about and/or watch death, deep-seated corruption, state-sanctioned violence, war and famine, discrimination, the failures of the government and the failures of everyday people. We read about people losing jobs, losing homes, losing family, losing faith. We watch people argue proven truths and dehumanise the experiences of our lives and our friends' and families' lives ... and then we respond by sharing some bits, donating some money, maybe shouting at a stranger, and going back to work or dinner or TV like nothing has happened. And that's on a regular day.

Too much information is a real thing. And living with what you witness online and not having any coping mechanisms sometimes feels like a new, very toxic, norm. There are plenty of critics of the 'too much information' argument, mainly people in your Instagram and TikTok feeds, telling you not to look away from the internet just because it's upsetting. And they have their points. Should we really be able to feel carefree in a world this gruesome? Should we really be able to see all that and then lock our devices and switch off? Tune into another episode of *Outback Opal Hunters*? If the internet connects us, then maybe it should connect us; wake us up each morning with a blunt and chilling reminder that people are suffering and there's a lot we don't know. Is it time to accept that being horrified and confused is part and parcel of being online? That we don't just get to take the memes and run?

Maybe this kind of assault on our everyday peace is the tipping point, what it takes to mobilise the people privileged enough to do something about the squillions of global atrocities so many of us comfortably ignore.

It's important to remember that just being witness to the horror is not necessarily helping. Reposting and liking and commenting and sharing isn't detrimental; it's supportive and educational. But exposure can't be the end game. Part of finding satisfaction beyond our online worlds means taking what we do there offline and trying it on for size, making it fit or benefit the real world. Do we live what we post? Do our day-to-day actions stack up against our stories? Are we changing the world for the better, really? Are we really being radicalised to finally act? Or are we throwing content at the problem and calling it a day?

Being constantly online can also be painful because we're often exposing ourselves to being bullied by our 'betters'; people with more money, more friends, more self-love, more personalised Louis Vuitton luggage. And whether our Higher Selves mean to or not, we compare what we've got with what we see. We probably spend more time than we'd like to admit watching these other lives that live in our screens, stacking them up against our own. Cooler, smarter, funnier, more privileged. More employed, more organised, more tidy, more snatched, more desired. We save posts and screenshots in the hopes that, one day, we'll have something a little closer to what they have; that these bits of content will somehow make us different. One thing that sets social media and internet envy apart from regular, everyday envy is that there's so much more to feel inferior about. And it's so much more frequent. In a world without our phones or computers, we might envy a few friends or a disgustingly blessed person we went to school with. We might envy our siblings because people are always complimenting them on their impressive job or sports game at family get-togethers. We'd maybe think of this resentment occasionally and complain to a friend about it over drinks, but it probably wouldn't consume us, or even live inside us all the time, because we'd only be reminded about it now and then, and there'd be thousands of opportunities to be distracted from it and be swept up in our own lives.

On Instagram, most of us follow a mix of people we know, people we almost know, Instagram celebrities, real celebrities and a bunch of accounts that post '80s bathrooms or fields of cows. When we first get online and sign up for an account somewhere, we're likely to start out following a few people we know in real life. Over time, that following list becomes more about who you want to see more of, which naturally tends to be things we're attracted to or impressed by.

Being exposed to the everyday lifestyle of somebody like Kylie Jenner – whether because you follow her or because she's unavoidable – is an experience most sane people would struggle to walk away from without at least a tinge of bitterness. The mansions, the cars, the closets, the babies dressed in head-to-toe Gucci. And she's just one account. Every day, we witness this kind of thing. People whose wealth is beyond comprehension, whose privilege is infuriating. Which surely can't be good for us. We follow people we look up to or are fascinated by, and so we end up being constantly reminded of what we don't have and who we aren't. Writing lists or speaking out loud about the things you love in your life can help with the account envy, even when it feels cheesy or forced.

I've lost the ability to retain NEW MEMORIES. I've never had a GOOD memory, but I used to remember, say, what I did the day before MOSTLY *

Ashley Feinberg

I think people quit
Twitter altogether
because we are in one
big room having a lot
of conversations that
require very different
tones and moods, and it
takes a lot to have them
SIMULTANEOUSLY

Darcie Wilder

Maybe you love your friendships, your pet, your job, or your neighbourhood. Maybe you sometimes forget how good you have it, how far you've come, how lucky you are or how hard you've worked for what you have. Maybe all this time online has meant that you've had less time to stop, look around and breathe it all in. Wake up in the morning and tell it to yourself in the mirror or the shower: *my life is good. I like myself. I am grateful.* By all means, scream into the ether about how hard you have it too, but remember that you're probably doing that a lot of the time anyway, maybe subconsciously. Your new task is to make room to appreciate the good bits. Strike that balance. And when you catch yourself tapping through stories of old friends and current acquaintances and thinking, 'Why aren't I at a party?', remember you're you, you're alive and the internet is only a half-truth.

When we're scrolling and bitter-watching each other, most of what we're seeing is the best of those lives – the highlights reel of the highlights reel. It's also the painstakingly curated version. We don't post our worst moments online for everyone to see, and even when we do, we edit them with our 'audience' in mind. We make them more palatable, more hopeful, more polished, funny and self-aware. We make sure that even if we're in the middle of a psychotic break, we're still adept enough to think of a clever caption, and we're still hot enough to not have entirely bird's nested hair. And it's not that we're being disingenuous, necessarily; many of us now see moments through the lens of how we'd post them. Here's my mental illness, and here's how I'd frame it. Here's my break-up, and here's how I'll announce it. Here's my annoying interaction at a post office, and here's how I'll live tweet it.

Looking at the events in our lives – or the feelings inside of us – from lots of different angles can be really revealing and therapeutic. But does this constant other voice thing ('How would I post about this?') mean that we're hardly ever just doing stuff? Living regularly and free of brain noise? Does it mean that we're

# ACTIVITY

How to stop comparing yourself to others

* **Make a note of what you're feeling.** Sit with it. Hate this picture? This post? This person? Feel it for longer than five seconds.

* **Notice and name the comparisons you're making.** Say them out loud or write them down. Get them out of the washing machine of your head.

* **Dig out your most knee-jerk insecurities.** What are you comparing? You might find that you're funnelling anger about unrelated stuff into this easy, more acceptable place. If so, why are you angry and what can you do about it?

* **Compliment yourself, baby!** Follow these bouts of subconscious self-loathing by telling yourself 'I'm good because …', 'I like myself because …'. Be nice to you.

* **Watch, read, look at or think about something you like.** Steer your train of thought elsewhere. There's no point letting it simmer and fester.

* **Next time, do it all again.**

already working on The Spin of each moment before the moment's even over? I don't know about you, but I've caught myself – many times – wording a caption in my head about something before realising I'm doing it. And I've built stories, filmed videos and drafted posts before discovering that I'm actually not ready to share that thing, and I might never be; I've just somehow reflexively ended up almost accidentally livestreaming my life. While there's nothing wrong with using social media as a tool for journalling, it can be meaningful to remember that your whole life doesn't need to belong to others, not if you don't want it to. Your thoughts, feelings and experiences can be private, just for you. If you so decide, a huge chunk of things that happen to you can live entirely offline.

One of the hardest things to stomach about being a person online, I think, is the regularity with which you're confronted by all manner of ideologies and points of view, and the casualness of all this information. Particularly hard to digest are the opinions that are chaotic or evil or untrue, and have real-world implications. Any normal day on a social media app will reveal thousands of fringe opinions about things you didn't know were even possible, and counter-arguments to things you were sure were not up for debate. The Earth is flat, the moon is simply not real and Louis Tomlinson's baby is fake. Nobody that's dead is actually dead – Elvis, Jeffrey Epstein, Tupac – and nobody who's alive is actually alive – Avril Lavigne, Megan Fox, Paul McCartney. The Earth is hollow, COVID-19 was made in a lab, Sandy Hook was staged, climate change is a hoax, Greta Thunberg is an actor, vaccines are poison, Hillary Clinton runs a paedophile ring, essential oils are a cure-all, Finland doesn't exist, the world is run by reptilian shapeshifters ...

The internet provides a place for these ideas to flourish, to propagate, to replace existing information and to spread like wildfire. Which is sometimes highly entertaining (convincing, even), but the result is a deeply fractured population that believes in all kinds of conflicting, polarising and radicalising realities.

Because various corners of the internet say they can and should. This can be a challenge to process, these millions of realities and beliefs being shoved in your face all day. And while it's likely always been a symptom of being a person on Earth, the internet brings these realities to your doorstep. No, closer. Inside your home.

The illusion of choice

As most of us are now very aware, the iPhone, its apps and their many peers are designed to be addictive; red notification bubbles that physiologically attract us, Autoplay and infinite scroll which keeps us plugged in, and the 'pull to refresh' function which intentionally mimics a poker machine lever. While these features were likely designed to make our lives sleeker and more interesting, they were also deliberately designed to pull us in and keep us there.

Tristan Harris was a design ethicist at Google before co-founding the Center for Humane Technology – and before being described by *The Atlantic* as the 'closest thing Silicon Valley has to a conscience'. He's also credited with inventing the phrase Time Well Spent and the resulting movement, which encourages makers and users alike to consciously adjust and examine our phone and device time. Harris has talked often about one of the major smartphone obscenities being the 'illusion of choice'. The iPhone's illusion of choice has us believing that it serves us the world in a rectangle. It knows everything and nothing is left out – or nothing that matters, anyway. When in reality, it knows bits and pieces and anything left out is expendable. While tapping through Tinder or browsing nearby cafés, we're encouraged to forget about what's not included. 'How many people that I might like to date aren't on this app? How many cafés that I might like to visit don't appear

 # ACTIVITY

How to be nice to yourself after a bad time online

---

* **Give yourself a minute.** It's ok to feel extremely upset by stuff you see online. Maybe it's hurtful to you personally, or just yuck content in general. Take the time to notice you feel bad and to stop what you're doing. You don't need to keep reading that article or scrolling the feed.

* **Break away.** Choose to do something else. It doesn't have to be offline, but it helps. Whether you close those windows or walk away completely, try changing the mood and the direction of the moment.

* **Self-care is important.** Wash your face or manicure your hands. Go for a run, change your sheets, keep writing that song or knitting that beanie. Do something to lighten the load and get out of the funk. Do something that can't hurt your feelings or piss you off.

* **Listen to music that uplifts you.** Put on a playlist that feels really good. Something bright, something fun. Or a podcast where you'll laugh a lot. Remind yourself just how good people can be.

on Google or Time Out or Broadsheet?' Behind the false narrative of 'collating everything', or the 'democratisation of information', the internet and the apps actually strip us of our ability to choose. When you can pay to promote a business, product or a point of view – either directly or via search-engine optimisation – browsing online becomes no longer autonomous.

We've been groomed to accept these colossal drawbacks to the online universe over years and years – our dependency, illusion of choice, account envy and the oversaturation of ideas – but it's time we start taking back some of our internet.

Are you there, God? It's me, and my arm hurts

Accepting that your phone hurts your physical body is the easy part. It's not hard to imagine, really, between the incessant findings that our bodies are evermore buckling, literally, under the pressure of our screen time. But taking that information and putting it towards new habits tends to feel, for some reason, more or less impossible. No matter how concise the infographic or shell-shocking the article, we still can't seem to make holding our phones in both hands and up at eye level feel anything but totally absurd. Consider this your official wake up call to do something about it, once and for all.

In 2014, Dr Kenneth K. Hansraj, Chief of Spine Surgery at New York Spine Surgery and Rehabilitation Medicine, conducted a study that showed when we bow our heads to look at our phones, they become a heavier strain on our necks. The lower we tilt our necks towards our laps, the more weight our necks have to carry. If your head upright weighs five kilos, when tilted forward fifteen degrees it's more like twelve, which is your head plus three bricks.

EXPLAINER

What's all this screen time doing to our bodies?

* **It's changing our ability to process emotions.** Many studies have shown that lack of face-to-face interaction, replaced instead with an increase in screen time, can lead to poorer social skills and a stunted emotional capacity. Experts recommend putting away the devices and spending more real time with real people.

* **It's shortening our life expectancy.** In 2011, a study of nearly five thousand adults indicated that excessive screen time increases our risk of death. The study also showed that participants who exercised regularly weren't any less at risk, suggesting that screen time itself is the issue, not just the sitting still or browsing.

* **It's making our vision worse.** Ophthalmologists recommend taking breaks from our screens every ten to fifteen minutes and have, the world around, warned that prolonged screen time can lead to eye strain, impaired vision, pain and worse.

* **It's changing our actual brains.** Too much time in front of a screen (yes, even when it's interactive) is capable of changing the very matter of our brain. In a study published in 2013 by Heidelberg University in Germany, researchers found that participants with 'smartphone addiction' had less grey matter – the part of the brain that processes information.

When your neck is titled forty-five degrees downwards, your head might as well weigh twenty-two kilos, or, your head plus two bowling balls.

If we're spending 3.5 hours a day on our phones, that's one full day a week we're putting a strain on our necks and backs. Almost two months of every year.

The just-about worldwide habit of leaning our heads forward, day in and out, until we sustain permanent injury is what they now call text neck. It causes neck pain, shoulder pain, back pain, headaches. Stiffness, tightness and a more forward-leaning posture.

But text neck – and text back and text thumb – aren't the only afflictions we're suffering from thanks to our devices. We're also experiencing dry eyes (in droves), sore eyes and blurred vision. Nerve damage, muscle damage, disc compression or herniation, headaches, early arthritis, numbness, depression, loss of lung capacity, and likely worse. After all, we're only fifteen years into having smartphones.

Me? Three years ago, I woke up and couldn't move. Unable to sit up or even turn my head on the pillow while lying down, I was frozen. Something had gone wrong in my back. I lay there, sort of planking involuntarily for a while, my anxiety mounting. By 10 am, I had unfrozen enough to text someone, and by 11 am, enough to wriggle loose and free myself like Michelle Pfeiffer in *What Lies Beneath*. Then into the shower, into some clothes and off to work in an Uber, crumpled up in the backseat like an old receipt. I felt basically fine until lunch, when my neck seized up again, and so I'd waddled out of work to an appointment. In the office of a myotherapist I'd never met before, I was firmly told, 'You have to use your phone way, way less.'

It seemed absurd that I, a spritely-ish twenty-eight year old, a well-enough person, a person with *dreams* and *desires*, should end up incapacitated just from having an iPhone and looking at it a huge amount. But I decided to hear him out anyway.

After my appointment, I began to notice little things about how I lived my life. I noticed that I usually held my phone near to my lap or on an angle so that my head was always twisting to meet it. I noticed that it was normal for me to lie in bed with my laptop on my stomach, my chin resting on my chest. I also noticed that it kind of hurt. (Had it always been this way?)

I held my phone too far away from my face, too close up, too tilted, too bright, too dim. I'd crush my phone-holding arm underneath myself on the couch on my side, reading forty-two-part threads on Twitter while I cut off the blood to my hand with my body weight. I got tiny cramps running between thumb and pinky when I scrolled the apps, and a dent in my palm that the corner of my phone made after a session. A sore shoulder, headaches, sore eyes, and I noticed how long it took me to get to sleep at night.

I started thinking *Why did I get this big phone instead of the normal one?* and *Do I always scrunch my shoulders up like this when scrolling?* And what the hell is wrong with me? After a little while of properly paying attention, I also began to notice minute spasms in my lower back which didn't feel new. I'd probably just never picked up on it before. Then tingles down the back of my right arm, along my elbow and forearm and into the right side of my hand. Aches in the upper-middle-ish of my back. A kind of tightness in the right side of my neck. Soon, it was impossible to ignore how painfully inconvenient this item was, and yet ... here we were. Best friends, inseparable. Madly *in love*, you might even say.

These aches and pains and mutations were the body's way of saying, 'Enough, idiot. You haven't figured it out on your own yet, so here it is: undeniable proof. This thing needs to go.'

I won't lie to you; I never intended to part ways with my phone over this. But I also wasn't entirely sure that I'd ever change anything at all, not even the worst habits. For a few weeks after the appointment, I kept using my phone as I always had. Why? Because it was fun! And everybody else was doing it! Even when my arm

ACTIVITY

Ways to break out of sleep scrolling

⁎ **Move.** Do something with your body. Move away from your devices. Hang your head between your ankles or stretch your arms up at the sky. Circle your head around clockwise and anticlockwise. Move whatever limbs you can. Get the blood pumping and let your body feel something.

⁎ **Make noise.** We can forget how quiet we are while scrolling, searching and gaming, how even our laughing is mostly silent, just barely observable snorts of air. Make some noise for a change! Sing along to music you like, call a friend and talk loudly, or just say stuff to your pet or plants or whatever. And try doing it without turning it into content.

⁎ **Use that beautiful brain.** Do a quiz or a test, watch an educational YouTube tutorial or a mini-doco. Do something that actually requires your attention, but not much from your hands. You don't even have to get off your phone or computer, just break up the monotony.

⁎ **Listen.** Just stop and sit or stand quietly. Close your eyes and pay attention to the sounds and movements around you. Sink into your couch cushion or your patch of grass and take a moment to pay attention to the world moving around you.

⁎ **Be real-world social.** Go and see another person. Sit across from them and hear them speak. Buy them a coffee. Tell them your thoughts. Ask how they're feeling. Let the unbridled goodness of IRL human connection get to you.

tingled or my neck hurt, I wouldn't do the exercises or even put down the phone. I thought *maybe it'll go away by itself.* And I might never have done anything differently at all if not for the shiatsu masseuse I encountered one rainy weekday morning who asked me, nonchalantly, at the beginning of a session, 'So when did you break your back?'. I was humiliated enough to finally make some changes.

Very slowly, I forced myself to try habits recommended by doctors, therapists and Instagram gurus alike: holding your phone in both your hands, holding it right up to your face and taking breaks to twirl your neck and arms around at intervals. Stretching, closing my eyes, turning my phone all the way off and charging it in a room far away at night.

These new habits slipped and fell by the wayside all the time, and still do. In fact, there have been times where I've caught myself on my phone, in a contorted position on the couch while half-watching the TV and also clenching my teeth, writing a passage for this very book. About the insidious nature of unconscious device use.

But more and more, these habits become a part of me and who I actually am. I choose to do them because I care about myself and am afraid of becoming a giant mollusc. (I sometimes have to remind myself, out loud, of this). And I continue to do them because I now see the relationship between the exercises and a better quality of life. So, between phone use and computer use, and as often as I can be bothered (which is more and more all the time), I stretch, I move, I adjust for new angles. When I notice that soreness coming around in my palm or a sting in my little finger or an ache in my shoulder, I know it's time to get up. Put the phone down and close the computer. Move around and try using my body in a different way.

Stretches, exercises and breaks from devices will genuinely make the difference between becoming a pretzel and not becoming a pretzel somewhere down the line (no, I don't know when). Find ways to build these new habits into your life the way you'd build anything else into it, like waxing, sit-ups, cutting your nails.

* When was the last time you slept for **10 HOURS?** 12? Sleep feels **GOOD**. And you're probably tired. **WHY NOT**, instead of scrolling, go to bed at 8pm?

Make them part of your daily or weekly routine until they're no longer an extra step you're taking, but something you can't imagine living without. The good news is that stretching and moving will, unlike most things that are good for future you, feel instantly gratifying.

Being good to your physical self

There are lots of other little and big things you can do for your body that will feel good and make your life better. Each one you add to your life repertoire will also, delightfully, replace time you might normally spend on your devices.

Take the time to appreciate your body; really think of it, acknowledge it and show it attention. Doing thoughtful things that don't involve scrolling and tapping or just staring at a screen will probably change the way you feel about yourself, and will also help you to mentally create a list of routines and practices that live totally – or mostly – offline.

Work on your core strength a few times a week – ever tried planking on a loved one? – and take baths to relax your muscles. Use Epsom salts and nice oils, really make a whole thing of it. Practice being in the bath with no distractions. No phone, no movies, no books. Just be. Challenge yourself to think about things that make you feel good, or plan for things you can get excited about. If you don't have a bath, take a plastic stool into the shower. If you don't have a plastic stool, just sit in there. Try new things in the shower, like eating fruit or drinking coffee. It's always nice to shake things up a bit. Nap! Just sleep more.

Go for really, really long walks. Ones around your neighbourhood or further. Walk until you don't know where you are anymore. Walk without your phone, without music. Be entirely alone and in the outdoors. The bonus with walks is that you'll see some world at the same time. People in their gardens and blue flowers dancing in the breeze. Birds and bugs and dogs and cats. You'll also get to smell some good smells, like cut grass and wet dirt and people barbecuing and crisp, fresh air. Good for the body and good for the mind.

Plant a garden! On your balcony, on the fire escape, on the verandah. Try growing a herb, a jalapeño plant, a native flowerbed or something for the bees. Adopt a dog, foster a cat, buy a few fish! Find something to care for that takes you out of yourself. Then do it again and again. Have a house full of plants? Get a few more.

Breathe. Just stand there and breathe. Moisturise your hands, and when they're sore or tired or just in need of attention, massage them, or ask someone else to. Lie down flat or sit however feels good for you and your body and give yourself a break. Close your eyes without sleeping, a criminally underappreciated joy.

Eat a piece of cake or a McDonald's apple pie. Make yourself your favourite drink – an iced coffee or a whiskey highball or a green juice – and drink it without doing anything else. Give yourself the space to actually enjoy it.

Think of the way you treat others and try turning that inwards. You deserve your own patience and kindness. Try embedding rituals of softness and caring into your life, ways to show yourself tenderness.

ACTIVITY

Ways to feel alive again

* **Call someone you love or like.** Tell them what you like or love about them.

* **Do something different to your hair or face or body.** New eyeshadow, new hat, new nail polish, new exercise routine. Remind yourself what it's like to feel new.

* **Watch an animated movie.** Movies made with kids in mind are pure and just. Bad people perish, good people (and good French rats) prevail. It's a nice world to live in for an hour or two.

* **Make something!** Make a bucket hat out of a towel or a tote bag out of an old tablecloth. Make a zine, paint some shoes, re-cover a cushion, write a song. Remember that your creativity is what makes you human.

* **Give back!** Volunteer, donate some money, help a friend move. Get out of your head and into the world, feeling useful and real and kind.

* **Do something you've been putting off.** It's not easy; that's why you haven't done it yet. But imagine how good it's going to feel when you have! Stop procrastinating, put aside some hours and finish that thing! Pay the bill, write the email, finish the project, confront the problem. Make a note of what you're going to reward yourself with and then follow through with that part too.

* **Scream.** Really loud. Maybe text the people you live with first, but then go for it. A good scream can really turn things around.

Chapter Four

WHO ARE WE online & what are we DOING THERE?

Because being online is so normal and posting is so second nature, it's easy to forget where our online selves end and our actual selves begin. Where are the gaps and gulfs between our online personas and our real-world selves? And where did they even come from? I first started drumming up an online falsehood in the late aughts, the days of MySpace, when I decided if I didn't work out how to be cool online, I would probably die of embarrassment. I lamented over display pics and which pop-punk songs were good enough to embed on my profile and I did this until my brain hurt. Online Me had to be cute, smart, funny, fake awkward, and a bit of an over-sharer but in a cool way like Lisa Crystal Carver. I wanted attention but mainly privately, and I wanted to feel like I wasn't just on the internet, I was in the middle of it, where all the good stuff was happening. All of these desires, as you can imagine, spawned a lot of disappointment. And I've done almost zero re-examining of that performance since.

I've never quite been able to shake that deep-down need to appear effortlessly smart and chill and funny online – which I don't generally suffer from when I'm not on the internet. Here's the thing: I hardly ever feel like I've achieved that veneer, and even worse is the guilt I feel for all the hours I spent trying to.

Just like we're different at work or in new relationships, we're different online. Because we can be and because it sometimes feels like we're supposed to be. But it's not like we log on and then pretend to be this person and log off; it's not 1999. We're different on TikTok, different again on Instagram and different again on Reddit. And we're all of these different things all the time, because the logging off doesn't really happen.

Being a bunch of different people all the time won't kill you, but it is acutely exhausting – and if you've ever had to code-switch for your own self-preservation, you'll know this well enough. Fracturing ourselves over and over just to feel at home online might mean that we're getting further away from who we are and what we're about. It also might mean that, later on, somewhere down the line, when the autumn years are upon us and we're looking back at the years passed, we might feel a bit like: *wait a second, why did I draft and re-draft so many comments and captions? What a colossal waste of my precious time.*

Just as it's easy to forget who we are online, it's easy to forget what we were even doing there in the first place.

Whether we choose to spend the bulk of our time posting in subreddits, commenting 'at this point I don't even know if I'm breathing right' on YouTube videos, sharing aesthetic photos of lambs and ducklings to our Instagram stories, or shitposting on Twitter, it's not often that we ask ourselves *why* we do it and what we get out of it, apart from it being generally fun and something to do. What's in it for us, other than quickening (and occasionally softening) the passing of time?

In all the hurry to get online, be good at it, monetise it and then somehow maintain the momentum, it feels like the point got left in our dust. Like maybe we lost touch of what we were actually trying to do there. Sure, we're connecting at lightning speed, but is it really making us closer? Or is it zapping some of the beauty from the offline world? Is the internet the information superhighway, or is it more like a house of horrors, where every guest should be wary of every corner, and treat every new bit of information as suspect?

Why do we post? Why are we on there so often? What's it all about? Do we need to practice second-guessing our instinct to do it? What do we want, aside from something to soothe the fear of missing out (FOMO)? Or worse, knowledge of missing out (KOMO)? Aside from replies and comments and likes and retweets?

Aside from a bit of attention? A place to put our thoughts and feelings, a place to catalogue our lives?

Just as we should think about auditing the content we consume, we should take some time to think carefully and critically about the content we share. What kind of person am I to follow? A positive person? Do I educate? Do I use what platform I have for good? Do I want to? Do I amplify others or do I monopolise the space? Do I connect with people or do I project? Do I respond to stories just to hear back?

When I began auditing my online presence, it quickly became clear that I had been posting for attention: to be liked, approved of, thought of and admired, at a stretch. As deeply depressing as it may sound, the dormant, underlying drive behind almost everything I did online was validation. I was dependent on likes and comments and replies. Because somewhere along the way, I'd decided that being actively recognised online truly meant something about my worth as a person. This meant that sometimes a post or a video or joke took hours to create – in my bedroom, by myself or with friends, while we got later and later for real-world engagements. The time was justified because the pay-off was so big: feeling good about myself.

I didn't form this dependency because I lacked attention elsewhere. I had good friends, an okay job, a fun social life, a busy sharehouse. But the pull of online validation was, for some reason, greater. I'd been more or less content and relaxed in real life, but the more I tried to cultivate a personality online, the more neurotic I became about how others saw me. Did they like me? Did they want to hang out with me? What was the difference between me, and all those people with fifty thousand followers?

When people liked what I posted and gave me the responses I hoped for, the rush of attention and validation was good, but my expectations only grew more unreasonable. If three hundred likes was my personal best, I wanted more. And the thrill never lasted

* **What is actually worth being POSTED online? And what is the thing that COMPELS us to do it?**

that long. The likes felt good for a few seconds, the comments a little longer, especially if they were highly complimentary, but once the activity stalled and the rush was over, I'd have to cling to that faint buzz of relevance, tightly, until it faded a few hours later. *I posted something good*, I'd feel, until it was time to do something else. What was worse was that my obsession meant collecting the likes and comments in their *numbers*. I wouldn't see the notifications as real communications from real people – some I had known and loved for more than twenty years – I saw them as data.

The casino of going online

What qualifies as 'addiction' to internet use and devices varies, so the statistics of people worldwide who are addicted are wobbly; somewhere between 1 per cent and 8 per cent. But what does addicted look like? Being online constantly? Roughly three in ten Americans believe they're online 'almost constantly', according to a survey conducted by the Pew Research Centre, and the average Australian spends more than five hours a day online.

Compulsive online or device use doesn't just fall on people who absolutely adore going online. Some are more likely to be more obsessed than others. For example, people who are predisposed to addictive behaviours, or who identify as addicted to the internet, are more likely to experience depression, anxiety or to have ADHD.

According to researchers, there are five identifiable kinds of internet and device addiction; gaming addiction, compulsive information seeking, addiction due to online relationships, addiction to cybersex or porn, and addiction to what they call 'net compulsions' – online shopping, gambling, trading stocks and online auctions. Hilarie Cash, an expert in internet addiction and recovery, writes, 'The Internet functions on a variable ratio reinforcement schedule (VRRS), as does gambling. Whatever the application (general surfing, pornography, chat rooms, message boards, social networking sites, video games, email, texting, cloud applications and games, etc.), these activities support unpredictable and variable reward structures.' More importantly: 'The reward experienced is intensified when combined with mood enhancing/ stimulating content.' In other words, we're being doubly duped. Sure, the content is addictive – staying current, feeling included – but so is the very act of checking.

For my compulsions (checking, checking, needing attention, checking), I found that I needed to post less to break the cycle of needing validation and reward. If I took longer breaks from the attention, I'd crave it less and find returns elsewhere. Which, so far, feels more real and more liveable. And much less brain-occupying.

This won't necessarily be true for you. Maybe for you, the support and love you receive online is better than what you receive offline. Maybe you rely on it in a way that really means something, and the stuff you post is completely, authentically you, and you can truly say that you're just expressing yourself. Or maybe you don't know what you're doing online yet, you're still figuring it out and you're ok with that.

The answers to why you're doing what you're doing online will be totally unique to you, but they'll almost definitely reveal one common thing: what we do online is more insular than we thought.

Because of our propensity to minimise stress and risk in finding comfort zones, most of us are using the internet in a wildly limited way. Whatever you use the internet for, and wherever you spend the majority of your online hours, you're likely spending the bulk of your time in some pretty niche places. While the Twitter timeline and the front page of YouTube don't always feel that niche, we know they are, because we know that what we're seeing is just one permutation of one platform in the vast infinitude of the internet. Spending all our time in these cosy corners isn't

ACTIVITY

How to make your internet use more you-ish

---

* **Mix it up. Take a week and post less.** Then post more the week after. Try sharing more content by others if you're usually creating your own. Then flip it; try posting all your own stuff instead.

* **Give over-sharing a go!** Being more vulnerable, expressing yourself, letting your online world know a little more about you. Try to do it earnestly and without irony. If you're usually sincere? Try switching it up. Take a load off, challenge yourself not to share so much. Try enjoying the internet as a spectator for a week.

* **Change your routine and your safe spaces.** If you're usually knee-deep in Instagram, head on over to YouTube for a bit. Take a look around. Addicted to TikTok? Spend some time on Reddit. Try new games, read new publications. Push yourself to experiment and get to know some new corners.

* **See what's out there.** Head to the search engines and manually look for new things to get into. See what else is out there and try actively getting to know the internet better; what don't you like? What do you? Make some mental notes.

necessarily all bad, or bad at all – we form communities and we find belonging. Still, it can sometimes feel like ordering the same meal at the same restaurant every night – a nice, comforting routine that leaves little room for joy or surprise and, in lots of ways, shrinks the world we live in.

Don't let it break you (if you can help it)

Very much interwoven into the fabric of being online is having an opinion; feeling like you either need to add your thoughts and feelings to the discussion, or echo the thoughts and feelings of those you respect. The size and speed of posting and news online has meant that forming an opinion about something has become less about being thoughtful or educated, and more about being the most right, the most quickly. Having the Most Perfect Opinion. While forming an opinion about something usually requires having a grasp of the concept and a varied list of sources, online it generally only calls for an active account. We see something, we think, we post. Repeat. This phenomenon sucks, for lots of reasons. It's too loud, too much, too obnoxious, too competitive. And it often means the opinions about a topic drown out the original topic, so that nothing really ever sinks in, or no conversation is ever led to its logical end. It also begins to feel like one of the principle exhilarations of the early internet – posting wildly because life was chaos – is a long-dead pipe dream. Being convinced we know everything (just because we're online and we read stuff) doesn't just make us insufferable and obnoxious. It also leads to us being constantly wrong, and feeling attacked when we're corrected, or mocked for it.

If you're hoping, expecting or planning to live a life on the internet where you're constantly adored, get out now. Log off and become the North Pond Hermit because if you're posting, you're going to do things that people absolutely hate. Not because there's anything necessarily wrong with you, but because it's How It Is. When you're sharing your point of view with the world, there's always going to be somebody who wants to scream about it. If you're unlucky enough, you may even find your point of view being shared and mocked with virality, jeered at by possibly tens of thousands (though we're more likely to be one of the tens of thousands, aren't we?). This is unavoidable because the internet has empowered us all to dust off a wooden box, stand on it and shout our silly little opinions at anyone who'll listen. And sometimes, those opinions are insane. We're all going to end up in conversations where we're out of our depth, and asked questions we don't know the answers to, and we're going to answer them because we want to sound smart or like we care about stuff. And we're all almost certainly going to say some things that are misinformed or insensitive or just plain foolish. Or, because it's the internet, you might say something as regular as 'Elmo seems nice' and wake up one morning to find you've lit a fire of rage inside of strangers all over the world, inspiring Buzzfeed polls and podcast episodes and think pieces in *The Guardian*. However it happens, you will, at some time, go online and be told you're 'wrong', 'stupid' and have 'worms for brains'. And some of the time, The People will be right.

Spoiler: it doesn't feel good to be called wrong or stupid or to be corrected by what feels like everyone, or to be the butt of jokes. But learning to cope and 'grow' from it will take some of the sting out. First, best to get rid of that inner voice that tells you that being wrong is bad. It's not, and it's not just because it's not reasonable to expect to be right all the time, but also because being right about everything is kind of annoying.

Being a person is a learning curve, so when we say something that elicits anger or pain or criticism, the first thing we should do is listen. Hear the critics out, think it all through, and do our research.

Fracturing ourselves OVER AND OVER just to feel at home online might mean that we're getting FURTHER AWAY from who we are and what we're about ✳

Then, we should find out just how wrong we are, how we can be less wrong and start thinking about making amends.

Second, we can avoid the easy slip ups that lead to Being Wrong In Public by trying to post more conscientiously. The more we post on a whim, the more likely we are to say things or share things we don't totally understand the implications of. And the more we post in the hope of being praised and More Correct, the more likely we are to be dunked on by the next More Correct group of people. Before we repost something or give our opinion, we should all make it a habit to just ... wait. Break away from the urge to be first, or early, or the loudest in the conversation, and dig deeper instead. Read sources we trust, see what the particulars are and inform ourselves the way we would if we were sharing or promoting something *offline*.

Ask yourself a few questions before posting or sharing something online: What do I *really* know about this? What are the ethics involved? Will I have answers if people have questions about this? What am I trying to achieve? Who am I trying to connect with? Am I inadvertently piling on with the tens of thousands for sport?

 # ACTIVITY

How to be wrong about stuff

* Practice saying, 'I haven't heard about this', 'I don't know enough about this' and 'I need to learn more'. There's no harm in admitting where there are gaps in your knowledge.

* When you're challenged, check yourself on your instinct to push back and get defensive. Even when you're being misunderstood, there's probably something new to learn. Take a few moments to process things and try to let go of the compulsion to be absolved. Being wrong is fine.

* Ask for more information. Or, if it's something you can learn on your own without having to ask, do some googling. Take the time to educate yourself.

* If you're up to it, thank the people in your life who are taking the time to politely educate you. Explaining things to people takes time and energy and patience. When people are patient with you, let them know you appreciate the help.

* Normalise expressing an interest in something without having to add your opinion or your take. Not everything is about how you feel.

* Read reputable sources. This means sources that cite their sources. Publications that fact-check. Follow people who link to resources and make distinctions between their opinions and empirical knowledge.

* Listen! (refer to How to Listen in Real Life on page 118)

# ACTIVITY

How to get some privacy back

* **Change your passwords regularly** and make them super hard to crack. Make them long and full of numbers and symbols. Make them so good that not even you can guess them, then download a password manager to keep track of them all.

* **Use a secure messaging app** like Signal or Wickr where your messages are encrypted end-to-end, meaning totally private.

* **Disable the personalisation of ads in social media apps** and in your device's settings. In order to cater online marketing to you personally, companies need to mine your data and monitor your activity, which is gross.

* **Try not to store sensitive or important information on drives** like Google Docs and Dropbox. Take your scans of documents like your birth certificate and your list of passwords and save them to a folder on your desktop.

* **Check in on the permissions settings in each of your apps regularly.** When that little box comes up in the middle of a browse, saying 'We've changed our terms and conditions' and you click accept because you're watching a stunning TikTok and you want to be left alone – time to go and check in on that. Head to your app settings on your device and make sure you're comfortable with the level of privacy you've agreed to.

# EXPLAINER

Broadcasting ourselves

We're all aware that – when we're not monitoring our settings and being vigilant – going online and using our devices means handing over big chunks of our private lives, and agreeing to being consistently tracked. Both virtually, as we traipse across the various regions of the internet, and in the physical world, thanks to practically always being attached to a GPS.

But it's not just the phone company or the CIA agent watching through the selfie camera that we need to be wary of, it's our intended audiences too. When our accounts aren't on private, just about anybody is privy to what we post and share – employers, exes, family. And it's all too easy to forget how discoverable (and vulnerable) we are online.

Chapter Five

WHAT TO Do About The Apps

Do you remember a time when there were four apps? Snake, a music player, a ringtone creator and email? Me neither.

Now there's an app that sends you a notification a minute before it rains, an app that records you while you sleep talk, an app that makes a very loud beep when you press a button and does nothing else, and an app that – if you leave it open and nearby during sex – tells you how 'good' you are at it. Some would say that's too many apps. But the volume of apps is easier to accept when we remember we've been given apps as good and crucial as Shazam, Find My iPhone, Wickr, Google Translate, Cameo, and that one that tells you what plant you're looking at when you point your camera at it. Swings and roundabouts.

Most of us tend to collect apps like debris, clinging to us like trash around the ankles and making it harder to move. At least, that's how it can feel. This is why we should take the time to audit our apps. Delete apps you don't use, don't like, don't perceptibly benefit from. The ones you downloaded while tipsy, as a joke, or while so bored you thought you might pay four whole dollars for one, and in fact then did. Delete the apps that clutter your life and your mind, that give you cause to unlock your phone or swipe through your home screens, but then don't provide a real sense of accomplishment or meaning. Delete the pseudo self-help apps that make you feel bad about yourself, and the airbrushing, face and body altering ones that make you feel worse. Delete them because you're not learning that language and you're not doing that fitness regime. Pretend they're boxes full of old, broken stuff taking up space in your real-world home.

# ACTIVITY

Spring cleaning your home screen

Think about your phone's home screen as a place of minimalism and function. Here, you want to display the apps that actually serve you in your everyday life, the ones that get you from A to B, that tell you the weather and get you out of bed in the morning (Rideshare apps, banking apps, your calendar, email, Google Maps).

Then, move all the apps that encourage limitless browsing or browsing for pleasure to the second or third page of your home screen.

The purpose of this is to make falling into scrolling apps that little bit harder. So that you're not impulsively clicking into Instagram and TikTok as much, you're not seeing them each time you unlock your phone and you're not thinking of them as often.

What to do about social media

Depending on the day, the time and recent events, we're likely to think one of two things about social media. On a good day, they're a godsend, perfect, electrifying and worth their weight in gold. On a bad day, it's hard to believe they're even allowed. It's hard to believe that millions of people are allowed to send each other unsolicited messages and pictures the world over, about anything, for any reason. And yet, here we are. Instagram, TikTok, Twitter, Snapchat, Facebook, YouTube and their ilk are as exhausting as they are bewitching, as horrifying as they are comforting. It sometimes feels like social media has only made our lives more complicated, messier and lonelier. Worst of all (not really, but it sometimes feels like worst of all), all the apps seem to wish they were each other. Instagram adds Reels, Twitter adds Fleets and, eventually, it's as if we're just fragmenting ourselves among these platforms, posting the same stuff to each of them in some aspect, and living in a devastating mess of syndicated content.

Still, they occupy our lives to such an extent that we've changed our real-world parameters to meet their guidelines; we've changed our industries, our laws, our personalities and our definitions of beauty to fit what these platforms sell, proliferate and favour. Since the invention of the timeline or the feed, and the infinite scroll, it can feel like their presence in our day to day has no tangible end point … or point at all.

With nearly three billion active monthly users, the most beloved worldwide overall and the behemoth arguably responsible for it all is, of course, Facebook. A platform we once relied on to update our relationship statuses and wish each other happy birthday in droves, Facebook is now often considered one of the most contentious advancements in modern human history. The Wikipedia page specifically for 'Criticism of Facebook' runs over

23,000 words long. For perspective, that's almost as long as this book. For a little more perspective, the Wikipedia page for 'The Bible' comes in at less than 10,000 words.

Sure, Facebook was cool for a while; we got to make profiles and poke each other. But in the years since its advent, Facebook has made way for the popularisation and normalisation of all kinds of unfortunateness; catfishing, online stalking, ad fraud, fake news, facial recognition software, data mining, the 'like', cookie tracking, sponsored posts, targeting, 'engagement' and our now commonplace obsession with interpersonal comparison. All of which has been inflated times a billion by the unstoppable ballooning popularity of Instagram, an app that is at once wonderful (friends, direct messages, likes, nice photos, funny videos, going live, highlights, voting, AMAs, tutorials, filters) and unspeakably evil (influencers). So it stands to reason that a large chunk of the population is head-and-body-will-explode-if-I-don't-stay-on-it-permanently addicted. And still, many of us find that our time on Instagram is some of the most damaging of all our time spent online, to our lives and our self-esteem.

A place where people are paid to look good or be white or have money or be popular, Instagram can remind you, over and over, day in and day out, that you are lacking.

Algorithms applied in apps like Facebook and Instagram were designed to show us the world through a lens we liked and understood, by displaying content similar to what we'd already engaged with. And because of this, any dream that social media might, on the whole, subject us to broader horizons and unify us appears to be over. Our worlds are shrinking every time we use these apps. Click like, you'll see more of that thing. Comment and you'll be served similar content. Until, eventually, each of us is being served a miniscule little world of targeted nonsense online, all the while being told it's the world at large.

EXPLAINER

The feedback loop

Algorithms applied in apps like Facebook and Instagram were designed to show us the world through a lens we liked and understood, by displaying content similar to what we'd already engaged with. And because of this, any dream that social media might, on the whole, subject us to broader horizons and unify us appears to be over.

Our worlds are shrinking every time we use these apps. Click like, you'll see more of that thing. Comment and you'll be served similar content. Until, eventually, each of us is being served a miniscule little world of targeted nonsense online, all the while being told it's the world at large.

While the algorithms of Instagram once meant that our content was tailored to us, we have every reason to have lost all hope for learning and growing with Instagram, or any app. The codes determine our 'interests' by what we look at, or even pause for. So who we are and what we know is what they show us.

Because they're ubiquitous and I am enthralled, content featuring the Kardashians speckles the Explore section of my Instagram. I have seen less than five episodes of any of their shows, and only ever because it was already playing on TV, and I have never bought any of their products, nor followed any of them online.

I used to watch that content as it appeared in my feed, sometimes to see what they were *doing exactly* (also known as Keeping Up) but more and more as time went by, because I simply needed to marvel at them; the way their hips bloated outwards in instalments while their waists cinched inwards, and their stomachs only got flatter and flatter until the lines between torso and leg were all but annihilated. As a self-described half-believer, I gawked at the way they stole looks and trends from other cultures and communities and wore them like costumes, and gawked even more at the comments that congratulated them on these things, praised them for their perfection. I soon became addicted to seeing the things they chose to wear – which would then be marketed to me – and the ways that their forty-step makeup routines transformed them.

Because of this, and deservedly so, I am now served Kardashians content more than anything else. Because their wealth and cosplay mystifies me, I am considered, by the apps, a fan. I contribute to views on their videos, I make them more popular by simply witnessing them, and they, in turn, make more money.

This phenomenon of engagement equalling industry – also known as clickbait – where the number of views on a post justifies the making of another post in its likeness, because more views is *real life money*, crops up in millions of ways across the internet, each as bizarre as the last, and each as likely to throw you into an existential tailspin. A distant cousin of hate-watching TV, these Facebook craft, hack and prank videos feel less absurdly enjoyable or guiltily pleasurable and more enraging. And they might have never come to be if not for the patient zero of clickbait, headlines by Buzzfeed such as '16 Sassy Tweets From The Nation's 16th Largest School District' and '18 Potatoes That Look Just Like Channing Tatum' (both real, actual, yes, real headlines).

Because I've had a Facebook account, I've seen somewhere between fifty and five hundred DIY hack videos. It's hard to tell how many because they all use that one audio track. I've seen how to keep a bracelet in place with sticky tape, melt down a lipstick to fit inside a lip balm container, how to put a hoodie on backwards and eat popcorn from the hood. I can use a Sharpie instead of eyeliner, peel an apple faster by involving a power drill, turn an oversized jumper into a cocktail dress by cutting off, well, almost everything, and use two coins to pluck my eyebrows at work. 5-Minute Crafts, the most popular DIY video account on YouTube, ranks ninth for subscribers on the entire platform, with 67.9 million. That's six above Justin Bieber (15th). According to SocialBlade, 5-Minute Crafts makes somewhere between US$57,000 and US$900,000 a month, giving them potential earnings of US$11 million a year.

Content like this wastes our time, exploits our attention and impacts our *actual feelings*, turning otherwise harmless browsing sessions instead into fits of rage or moments of sheer bamboozlement. These videos are unsettling not just because they're not useful, but because they're *designed* to trick us into watching content we know isn't worth our attention, and they make *money* doing this. Wasting your time is their business model. Clickbait, and the insistence brands and accounts have on getting our attention and monetising it, is part of what is so confronting and depressing about being online. It often feels like each time the internet makes way for something truly great – a joke, a movement, a trend, an icon – there are only moments of glory before the brands and influencers cash in. This sucks because of capitalism, but also because it immediately ruins the good thing.

The content we love

Just as there are the accounts dedicated to clickbait content farming for money (hideous), there are, of course, the squillions of accounts we love that don't, for the most part, make any money out of it. Activists, comedians, educators, meme page admins and their hilarious, cool, weird, smart, free content. Let's be honest: they're the people who make the internet good.

There's a reason for the dreaded influencer boom and it's because running a popular account online is kind of a job. Just kidding, it's because everything good becomes co-opted by brands and corporations eventually. But, still. If you spend your life making stuff to put online and people absolutely adore it, you're likely, at some point, to start feeling like you deserve remuneration. And as easy as it is to scoff and eyeroll at the millions of people casually slipping the newest big brand matte lipstick into their latest post, or making merch out of a one-liner that went mini viral, there's only so much free content a person can be expected to make, particularly when their audience is absolutely huge.

A great reason to start thinking about paying your favourite content creators – or helping them get paid – is because, frankly, they probably deserve it. Being an online personality or running an account is work, particularly when you do it all day, every day. Normalising the idea that our favourite accounts – the ones that educate us, make us laugh, connect us, give us something to believe in – should be profitable is part of making the internet ours again.

 # ACTIVITY

Contribute to making the internet a better place

Choose a few accounts that really make an impact on your life, on whatever platform, and find a way to contribute to them. Maybe it's the blogger you've been reading since the first days of Tumblr, or the Instagram account that breaks down wellbeing practises using delightfully pastel infographics.

Find out how you can financially compensate them, it might look like subscribing to their Patreon or sending them a few dollars when you can afford it. Do what you can, and what feels right for you. If you can't afford to part with any money, there are loads of other ways to support your favourite accounts. Turn off ad blockers when watching your favourite YouTubers, or like, share and comment on your favourite account's sponsored posts.

Whether we're contributing to a Patreon or a Venmo because we want to see less sponsored content, or if we're engaging with the sponcon so our favourites can get paid, we're making a positive change. Because we're telling creators that we value what they do, and we're telling the 5-Minute Crafts of the world to get stuffed.

Just as we learn to weed out the clickbait and block out some of the evil monetising of the internet, so should we try normalising, in our everyday lives, the idea of paying for content that makes our time online meaningful.

Choose a few accounts that really make an impact on your life, on whatever platform, and find a way to contribute to them. Maybe it's the blogger you've been reading since the first days of Tumblr, or the Instagram account that breaks down wellbeing practises using delightfully pastel infographics. Find out how you can financially compensate them, it might look like subscribing to their Patreon or sending them a few dollars when you can afford it. Do what you can, and what feels right for you. If you can't afford to part with any money, there are loads of other ways to support your favourite accounts. Turn off ad blockers when watching your favourite YouTubers, or like, share and comment on your favourite account's sponsored posts. Making the internet a place where people can actually make a living without having to beg or peddle flat tummy tea is the goal.

Audit who and what you follow

There will come a time in every social-media user's life when they will stop, mid-scroll, and stumble upon a frightening realisation. Maybe on the train platform in the morning, or looking out your bedroom window into a lamp-lit street, you'll be suddenly awash with the knowledge that you follow a bunch of accounts that you simply despise.

ACTIVITY

How to stop brands making money from your views

* **Browse incognito.** Using an incognito browsing window or tab won't just protect your privacy, it will also change the way the internet markets to you. Without the data that informs their targeting, you'll be less likely to see more of the stuff you accidentally (or intentionally) pause on and don't want to see again.

* **Add a clickbait-blocking extension to your browser.** Chrome extensions like Clickbait Killer, Stop Clickbait, Anti Clickbait will work similarly to ad blocker extensions, identifying clickbait and removing it from your browsing experience.

* **Manually block bad brand content.** Use the drop-down menus on Twitter, Facebook and Instagram to go one further and block the accounts that post clickbait and co-opt our internet. This will also feel therapeutic.

* **Report and dislike content.** This, unlike blocking or hiding, will inform the creators of this stuff how you feel. In an ideal world, this would mean they eventually change their approach.

It's an important milestone in a person's life – realising that we hate-follow somewhere between five and one hundred accounts – and it's going to be a little shocking. Because once you notice just how many there are and how they really make you feel, you'll never be able to go back. But don't worry; there are paths to recovery.

Start by going through your accounts and looking at who you follow. Who and what are they? What do they post? What purpose do they serve in your life? How many of these accounts do you never even see thanks to the curs-ed algorithms? How many of these do you no longer care about? Who and what was a follow from ten years ago and no longer resonates? Who or what do you follow because it's bad or embarrassing and you like to make fun of it? Who do you follow because you're afraid to unfollow? Are there people and accounts you don't recognise? Are there people and accounts that make you feel bad about yourself? Do you compare yourself to strangers and end up in a funk? And most importantly: who and what makes you feel good? Which accounts are a source of comfort and pleasure? And why aren't there more of those?

Instagram has made culling your follows super easy by creating a category in your following list called Least Interacted With. Go in and see who no longer needs to live there. You might find that there are skinny, rich Danish 19-year-olds who pose in front of old European buildings in their oversized coats and they no longer need to live here. There might be ex-colleagues who post Infowars cutdowns who no longer need to live here. Friends you've fallen out with, meme accounts that are no longer funny. There might be accounts that once meant something to you that just don't anymore. Be honest with yourself and try to remember that online is not the whole thing. It's just one little part. The consequences won't be enormous. Culling these follows will feel good, more honest and less cluttered. Do this and then apply it to every social media account you have. Auditing who you follow begins with why you're online. Are you there to catch up with real-life people? Are you there to grow and learn?

Need help taking a break from *SOCIAL MEDIA?* Delete the apps for a bit and visit them on your computer browser *ONLY.* You'll do much less habitual checking this way and the user-unfriendliness of the interface will mean you're **LESS LIKELY** to stay plugged in

✳

Try making a *
private Instagram,
Twitter or TikTok
account where you
acquire exactly
ZERO followers.
Keep it totally
private, then post
there and see what
happens

According to a study by the University of California, Irvine, it takes an average of 23 minutes and 15 seconds to get back to that DEEP FOCUS on a task once you've been DISTRACTED *

# ACTIVITY

How to diversify your feed

* **See who and what other people follow.** This is the easiest and fastest way to find new accounts to follow and new worlds to explore. Go to your ten most treasured accounts on Instagram and Twitter, see who they follow, click through, look around and see what speaks to you.

* **Write some lists about things you've seen online that have changed you** or just made you feel really good (mini food, hair tutorials, local politics, ASMR, self-help). Go in search of more of that.

* **Write more lists about what's missing from your online life,** even if you're making stuff up and you have no idea if it exists. Create the world you want to live in. And go in search of that. Doesn't exist? Why not create it?

* **Use Google to find new people to follow** by searching things like 'best Instagram accounts 2021' and going to young, internet-y, switched-on publications for tips.

* **Look at who and what you follow and ask yourself if it's diverse.** Does this content reflect the world? Or does it look and sound mostly like you? Make sure that your feed isn't just tonally diverse, but diverse in perspective and expertise (no need to subject yourself to content that makes you feel bad or unsafe, though).

* **Ask your friends to send you lists of their favourite things online,** their favourite accounts and favourite bits of content. Add whatever speaks to you into rotation.

What about the social media worlds you love, want to change, and how do you want to feel when you scroll through the content you've chosen to see? When you're scrolling through the feed, are you disengaged? Waiting for something good to happen? Why not make your feed a place of All Good Stuff? What's stopping you from totally renovating your online worlds?

Go back to any lists – mental or otherwise – you've made about what kind of online life you'd like to have and apply it to any following or unfollowing you do.

Because online stuff can push us to our very limits, there will be times when you delete your favourite apps or disable your accounts altogether, which is a great idea. Taking time out from apps like TikTok and Instagram – the ones you never intend to fully delete, but periodically despise – is key to a happy life. Try to normalise deleting and reinstalling your apps, even just within yourself. There's no shame in sometimes wanting things and other times not.

Muting, blocking and soft blocking

If you were born after 1995, it's highly likely that muting and blocking is second nature to you; it's as much a part of the fabric of social life as following or tagging or sharing. If you're older, though – or perhaps just a little more anxious – it can feel like a lot. Dramatic, unnecessary, mean. You might feel like a person would have to really cross a line to get muted, and really, really cross a line to get blocked. (Like, for example, murder you and every single person you know).

But maybe it's time we all held hands and admitted it; muting and blocking needs to happen. Going online doesn't have to be an act of philanthropy, it can be whatever you need it to be.

For a long time, social media apps felt like a place you went, a room you walked into. You could customise your feed by who you

If the channels were to mysteriously vanish one day, are you going to be **FULFILLED** with what you've been doing for YOURSELF? *

Donté Colley

Perfectly good reasons to stop following an account:

* It makes you feel bad about yourself.

* It annoys you.

* You only follow it because everybody else does.

* It meant something to you once.

* It triggers you.

* The comments are upsetting.

* It bores you.

* You only followed back to be polite.

followed and unfollowed, of course, but if you followed someone, they appeared in your life daily (or however often you checked in). That is to say, if you were connected online, there they'd be. With the advent of the coded feed, which brought more 'relevant' content to the top rather than more recent, we're now looking at certain profiles and content more than we'd like to, and more than we should feel obliged to.

Who you follow online is often a delicate balance. We're following friends, crushes, family, colleagues, people you met one time or had a relationship with once. That cousin of the family you stayed with in Copenhagen. And maybe the fact of the matter is that you don't need all that stuff served up to you every day. Contrary to what we've told ourselves, your social media feed does not need to be a reflection of your offline life, and your browsing time does not need to be a place where you're caught up on the lives of everyone you know, if you don't want it to be. It should – and can – be a place of respite, joy, white noise, relaxation, education, good jokes and silly videos.

We've been on social media for a while now, and I think we're more than ready to agree that there are degrees of internet relationship. Social graces can't be as basic as 'follow' and 'unfollow', 'friend' or 'unfriend'. It isn't that simple in real life, and it shouldn't be that simple online. Thankfully, the app functions are finally beginning to reflect that scope.

But there's etiquette involved in who you follow and why, which is why you can't just unfollow a close friend when their online persona is annoying you or why you can't just block somebody because seeing their face makes you feel stuff. But the levels of limiting your online engagement with an account or a person are also about safety, self-preservation, kindness, ease and your privacy. That's why there's muting, restricting, blocking, soft blocking and more kinds of limiting access.

Muting an account is a temporary solution to a temporary problem. And a very delightful one at that. Muting means you won't see any of the account's content, but you'll still technically be following, and whoever or whatever you've muted won't need to know about how you feel if you don't want them to. In short? It's time to normalise muting people you love.

The people we love can be annoying, or just annoying online. Sometimes the people we love post things that make us uncomfortable or angry, and sometimes the people we love take up more space in our online worlds than we'd like. Sometimes the people we love post arse pics accompanied by a heartfelt caption about a devastating tsunami.

If there are accounts that you follow that don't bring something positive to your day, but that you can't or don't want to unfollow or block, mute them. Mute them for a few weeks, a few months or indefinitely. It's literally *your* online space, and it should look and feel like whatever you want. Perhaps visit the page you've muted now and then to revisit whether or not you'd like to keep it muted. If you don't want the account to know you've muted them, sprinkle a couple of likes now and then before leaving and continuing to live your life.

Blocking is, of course, a more extreme measure. But no less necessary. Blocking amounts to unfollowing an account, forcing them to unfollow you, stopping them from being able to see your account, and removing them and, in some cases, mentions of their name or account from your feed. While accounts you block won't get a notification when you block them, they will be able to see you've blocked them if they know what that looks like, and they probably do. The blocking tool is handy for accounts you have no interest in interacting with. For example, if you are being bullied online, block. If an account is posting misinformation and you feel stressed or upset when you see it, block. If an account feels aggressive or predatory or just not respectful, block!

Just remember that blocking should probably be reserved for the people you don't want to hear from at all, in real life and online.

 # EXPLAINER

What to do when you're blocked by someone you love

First of all: condolences. Nobody is born with the knowledge of what to do when this happens, but there are ways to work through it without making things worse.

* **Be angry, sad or confused.** Be however you feel like being because this is a terrible feeling and you deserve to feel it if you want to. Don't tell yourself it's not a big deal or it's just the internet because, as we all know, the internet is a real place and online happenings aren't trivial.

* **Keep an open mind.** It might be an accident or something they come to regret. Don't go straight to punishing yourself or wanting to call them and scream. Try to remember that the world is a big place and things happen a lot. In a year, you might even be laughing about it.

* **Think about it with the roles reversed.** Why do you block people? How do you or would you feel towards an account you blocked? Would you want to be confronted? Would you want to resolve it or leave it?

* **Breathe.** Go for a long walk and talk it out with someone you trust. Go for another long walk and think about something else. Listen to a nice playlist and remind yourself that life is sometimes chaotic and cruel, and you often need to take it on the chin. Don't worry, it will most likely make you a better person in the long run.

* **Try to keep cautious optimism about one day being able to maybe fix it.** Don't hold your breath but leave room for repair. In the meantime, move on.

And if you're likely to see them in person some time, it might be good to prepare something you can say to express why you blocked them, if they ask.

If you don't want to block but you want to gently remove someone from your followers, soft blocking is a good option. Soft blocking removes a follower from your list which, in Twitter, requires blocking them for a moment and then unblocking them, but in many other apps like Instagram can be done by removing, which appears next to their handle in your list of followers. Soft blocking is a strange beast and while generally non-confrontational, could lead to some pretty tricky conversations down the line.

Muting, blocking and culling your social media circle is good for you. It's about defining what your online world is about, who and what you want to surround yourself with, and where your boundaries lie. It's also about preserving real-world relationships. Just because you love someone in life doesn't mean you love them online. And just because you hate someone online, doesn't mean you love them any less in person.

Living in a world where you're free to mute and block means you yourself will inevitably be muted and blocked, unless you're one of those lucky people with twelve followers on Instagram (a perfect life). Head's up: finding out you've been blocked or muted by people you love will feel awful. It will feel like being punched in the gut. You might even be privy to a small emotional spiral about *What did I ever do* and *Why was I ever born?* It's ok. You'll be alright. Try to remember that it's perfectly normal to be disliked by the odd person here and there, especially online. Remember that you're not for everybody – nobody is – and that everyone gets to choose.

* Cultural sharing is ancient. That the speed and relative borderlessness of the internet makes cross-platform, global dissemination seem like a consequence of tech is a **CONVENIENT AMNESIA**

Doreen St. Félix

Chapter Six

WHEN PUSH Comes To Shove

Push notifications, so called because they are pushed out to users from the back end of an app are, theoretically, good. Or at least they were, once.

Introduced by Apple in 2009, push notifications were designed to alert phone users to updates of interest to them specifically: *your* sports team won the big game, it's going to snow in *your* area today. They were an improvement, and most device users likely would have mainlined them if they could. In 2013, rich push notifications – notifications that include 'rich' media like photos, videos and music, and which generally are interactive – were introduced, which meant that users could simply tap a notification and deliver an action, replying to a text or playing a song without having to unlock your phone. These kinds of alerts meant we soon would become even more tethered to our phones, responsive to every low-frequency sound, every glimmer of light. Any reason was reason enough to check our phone screen in the hope of a notification.

Lots of quality research has found that notifications are extremely addictive. That, much like the experience of playing the poker machines, pulling your phone from your pocket or flipping it over to reveal the screen is taking a risk on an unknown reward. The result – which notifications and how many of them – releases dopamine in our brains just like the red bubble in Facebook and Instagram, and the pull-to-release refresh on Twitter. The more notifications, and the more right the notifications, the higher the dopamine release. So notifications are a gateway into checking, re-checking and checking again in order to feel good. But to what end?

The reason for rich push notifications has become increasingly murky. Yes, we're still notified when we're emailed, when we win the game and about the weather, but we're also being incessantly

In the absence of time to physically and politically **ENGAGE** with our community the way many of us want to, the internet provides a cheap substitute: it gives us BRIEF moments of pleasure and connection, tied up in the OPPORTUNITY to constantly listen and speak

Jia Tolentino

marketed to through the rich push notifications: *Try this app. We're having a sale. We, a corporation, miss you.* And, of course, tricked into unlocking our phones and spending more time in the apps.

While the general consensus is that notifications selling us stuff are bad and annoying, the general consensus about app activity notifications seems on the whole positive. Or at the very least, neutral. It doesn't seem like the masses lament them, turn them off, or whinge about them online that much. In fact, we appear to have come to a universal understanding that we should be notified in real time when practically anything happens; weather, messages, likes, comments, news, friend requests, snaps, mentions and when Rashid, who you haven't seen in at least four years, has 'posted an update'.

It's quite an incredible thing we've all come to accept, though not exactly inconceivable, seeing as it's been such a slow burn, such an insidious progression. From text notifications on our first ever mobiles, to email notifications on our desktop computers that dinged. CleverTap, who create push notifications so they would know, has said that the average American with a smartphone receives more than 45 push notifications every day.

I used to receive them all day, and not even in a good, feeling-popular way. Most of them were from brands reminding me of their existence, or inane games I'd played in moments of weakness, letting me know that extra coins were *50% off for 24 hours only* (!!!!). These notifications, despite their uselessness, created a deeper and more evil bond between my phone and me. Because my phone lit up or vibrated when I received them, I was soon conditioned to expect it to. I was Pavlov's dogged into anticipating them, and because of this, I paid the screen almost constant attention. Looking at it during classes, during phone calls, during dinners, lunches, birthdays, movies. Nothing was important enough to interrupt my phone-checking. I can safely say that for at least two years, I paid my phone more attention than I did anything else.

And I am not alone in this, with Pew Research finding that 57 per cent of teens feeling that they're generally expected to respond to notifications immediately, and 41 per cent of teens feel overwhelmed by the number of notifications they receive daily.

Sean Parker, one of the co-founders of Facebook, once said that the social media colossus was built to 'consume as much of your time and conscious attention as possible'. Surprising? No, not at all. Horrific to hear out loud or read in plain text? Absolutely.

In the same interview, Parker said that likes and comments were part of a 'social validation feedback loop' which deliberately exploited a vulnerability in human psychology. And Facebook devised and developed that strategy more than fifteen years ago. Five years before push notifications.

Here's the thing: push notifications are a scam. Not necessarily in the sense that they're deliberately trying to scam you – the idea that notifications are withheld and then drip-fed to users in the hopes that they spend more time in the apps has been raised, then debunked, then raised and debunked again – but in the sense that you've been brainwashed, by no one in particular but perhaps everybody in general, to feel that your phone deserves your immediate attention no matter what else is happening.

If you are anything like the average person, then you will know this particular hell and you will know it well. Notifications give you ever more reason to check that screen, pick up the phone, unlock it and get to work in there, where you'll do approximately nothing – reply to a friend's text or a co-worker's email before surrendering to the bottomless worlds of the various news feeds. Notifications – once a delightfully innocent human invention, the height of convenience and on-the-go vibes – are seemingly rewiring our brains.

Notifications are not something you need or even necessarily want in your life, and a good chunk of them are actually the Bane (from Batman) of your existence. Disabling notifications on

* Try going just one day with all notifications *TURNED OFF.* Give yourself the **SPACE** to be left alone by apps and the internet

the apps you hate and even the apps you love will significantly improve your quality of life. When you turn off the notifications, the notifications stop coming. When the notifications stop coming, you stop expecting them. When you stop expecting them, you stop thinking about it. The less time you spend thinking about (and ultimately using) whatever devices you love most, the more time there'll be for other stuff; walking in the rain, crying to sad songs, meeting new people.

Here are the apps I now get notifications from: iMessage and an app called Pocketbook that helps me budget. And that's it. In the nine months since I turned off the majority of my notifications, I've been perceivably happier, more present in the world and nicer to be around. And this, I'm sure, is because I now think of my phone way less.

There will be drawbacks; it's trial and error. Some notifications are essential and there will be people in your life who lament your slow responses. You need to find out what works for you. What feels essential? Where are your priorities? Which apps do you need to hear from? Whose expectations do you need to manage?

Muted notifications on texts worked for me for months, until I developed a shiny new addiction; one to the feeling of opening my inbox and seeing four or five unread messages. A totally fresh feeling. So I began to unlock my phone more and check my messages manually. Like a tick, really. Until one day I realised what had happened. So text notifications went back on.

# ACTIVITY

How to break through the fear of missing out

FOMO (and KOMO) are surely two of the biggest driving forces behind our obsession with going online; missing the big news story or the running joke or that video everyone is quoting. So how do we break free of it?

* **Write down or say out loud what you're afraid of missing out on.** You might find that what you're envying in the lives – and posts – of others, you actually already have in your life.

* **Figure out which part of staying up-to-date feels good.** Does it actually feel good or are you just obsessed with being involved? When exactly does it feel good? And is the trade-off (scrolling forever and ever and ever) worth it?

* **Try to remember that all those crappy feelings scrolling through social media can bring up** – yearning and self-pity and envy and resentment – are feelings that we should probably try to avoid where we can.

* **Practice savouring your own day to day.** Take the time to enjoy your food, your alone time, your leisure time and when you get to spend money on something you're excited about.

Intermission!

Drop your shoulders. Drop your tongue. Breathe in and out like you mean it.

Chapter Seven

PUT THE
Phone
DOWN

It sounds crazy, but stay with me. You've made it this far. I'm going to assume you'd like to put your phone down. At least sometimes. And you know what? Good. I'm right there with you. Here's how you do it: put it *down*.

I'm not a doctor, but I'm a device addict and this is not a joke. Putting it down is a real thing and it works. Just put it down.

At first, it was hard, which sounds stupid but it's true. Especially when watching TV, like *The Great British Bake Off* because fun, silly TV is the perfect time for a spot of scrumptious half-arsed phone use. But more and more, you realise that this actually isn't that good. In fact, it feels kind of bad. Putting your phone down, away and in other rooms will force you to sit with yourself. Sit with your shows, your movies, your books, your friends. It will force you to re-learn or re-relish the idea of being there.

It's not easy, breaking habits. It probably never ever has been, not even once in the history of all humanity. But if you're unhappy and you know it, you just have to.

Start by leaving your phone in another room. *Charge* your phone in another room overnight. Learn to put your phone face down when you put it down – so you don't see it light up – and just out of reach so you can't turn it over out of curiosity, boredom, obsession, etc. Put your phone in a bag and leave it there. Extreme? Or radical self-care?

Make your phone's wallpaper something hideously ugly which you simply hate to look at. Put yourself in a position to pay attention to other things. You won't get as bored as you think, and if you do, challenge yourself to do something about it that doesn't involve a screen.

You'll probably tell yourself, 'I need it'; I did. 'I can't turn it off, I need it. I need it for work, I need it in case, I need it to keep up to date'. I need it, I need it. Lies, lies, lies.

The narrative we've told ourselves about phones is untrue: we do not need them every day. We do not need them to communicate or to feel loved or to keep on top of things.

Telling yourself you need it for work? Sure. But don't use it for anything your computer can't do. Telling yourself you need it to be contactable? Turn off your data and tell everyone to call or text.

Prove to yourself, even as a little one-day challenge, that you can go without your phone. Not bringing it with you from room to room and trying not to think of it too much. Not because you're addicted – which you might be, but who are we to say? – but just so you can see that it's not that crucial to your everyday life. Need a recipe? Pick up one of those heavy, papery things. Can't remember that one lyric? Continue living your life; it's not that important. Worried that people will miss you when you're gone? Want to hear something even more terrifying? They probably won't even notice. The internet is so full of noise and busyness that one person dropping off the feed is hardly likely to register. Worried about what *you're* missing? Think of it like a droplet of water in the ocean; one day of no phone between thousands of days of phone. Besides, being unavailable is hot.

Do more things that don't involve the internet. The more you occupy yourself, the less likely you are to think of your phone and use it. Put yourself in situations where looking at your phone would feel weird or out of place; go bushwalking, swim laps at your local pool, ride a bike, go to the movies. Any habits or hobbies you can work on that don't involve your phone, tablet or computer will help. You'll be strengthening the bond between yourself and the offline world and, eventually, the internet might seem a bit less interesting.

There's something about reading on a device that's also trying to be 1000 other things. A **BOOK** is just a BOOK ✳

Jenny Odell

Let your mind do its thing

How often are you left alone with your thoughts? How often do you allow your mind to just run, not about errands or deadlines or the expectations of the coming days, but just about nice stuff? Fields of flowers, people you think are hot, where you'd like to travel, your dream home.

I remember being little and looking forward to bedtime, because when we turned the lights out and the house was quiet, it was time to think about whatever I wanted. Imagine myself any way, doing anything. Sure, sometimes I was imagining tongue kissing Shane McCutcheon – I was a teenager – but other times I was picturing a holiday, or a party, or a beautiful bedroom, or being friends with someone I liked. And that peace and quiet – that freedom to go anywhere – over the years has, depressingly, decayed. More accurately, it has been eroded by years and years of staring listlessly into the glow of my phone before bed, and letting it be my imagination for me.

Many psychologists and neuroscientists talk about boredom as a tool for cognitive development and personal growth; that sitting with our own thoughts makes us more creative, helps us sleep better, encourages empathy and gets us thinking about our goals and future plans. To deprive ourselves of boredom – and to deprive the brain of space to breathe – teaches us that life should be a never-ending series of happenings. Which likely leaves us feeling empty and lost when there's nothing to fill the empty space. Try to build in empty space for yourself between appointments and errands and social gatherings. Leave room between episodes of that show, or between dinner and going to the couch for a movie.

Excuse me while I get corny for a moment, but in the last six months, I've started daydreaming before bed again. Thinking not of the things I need to do first thing in the morning, or of what I did or didn't do in my last relationship that made it all go wrong, but of new bed sheets and trips down the coast and all kinds of futures I might have. Of things that calm me and make me feel good, and it's on these evenings that I fall asleep most quickly into a solid night's sleep and wake up feeling good. Surely that feeling is worth thirty minutes without screen time.

How to stop half-watching

One of the most delicious and despicable habits of people like you and me is the apparently insatiable urge to look at – or attempt to look at – two screens at once. Two screens that are playing or offering two very different forms of entertainment, simultaneously, on and on so that it begins to feel like perhaps your brain is splitting. And let's be honest with ourselves (it's just you and me here); it's sometimes three screens.

Not that there's anything wrong with that. Kidding! There definitely is. But what we can admit is that it's a very special kind of satisfying, for whatever reason – hideous greed? The fear of real thoughts creeping in during milliseconds of quiet? And it's probably not going anywhere any time soon. It just feels too good. But there are some ways we can curb its grossness. For example, if you know you're not going to be able to watch that show or that stream or that movie without also looking at your phone incessantly because you're just in one of those moods, then don't put anything on that requires your actual attention. Put on some reality TV or a movie you've seen before – something you can comfortably ignore. There's nothing more annoying than looking up from your phone and realising you've missed something integral to the plot and having to go back, at which point you miss it again.

If you're feeling like you need to be torn away from your phone or tablet and forced to focus on something, watch a movie or show

Try leaving your phone in another room before bed and taking the time to think NICE THOUGHTS before sleep. Make QUALITY time for you and your brain

with subtitles, so you can't look away? Put your other screens somewhere else and sit on your hands if you have to. Make it a challenge to not have the multiple screens for at least half of the week. If that's already your average, do less. If your average is one night a week, good on you. Keep the screen circus under control when you can – even if it's just to prove you can do it.

Learning to communicate again

Whether it's the billions of bits of information bouncing around in our heads or the niggling urge to check our phones to see what everyone else is doing, something is responsible for our terrible attention span. Which to most of us just feels like we can't sit still through a class or a workday, or that maybe we're a bit more frantic and disorganised. One of the other ways our worsening attention span manifests in everyday life is in our relationships and our connections to others. If our attention spans are weak, we're probably not that wonderful to be around. One of the important real-world skills we appear to be losing as a collective consciousness is listening. We're so used to distractions and boredom and filling the silence and the space with pictures and videos and chats and noise, we're getting progressively worse at just sitting and hearing someone speak. Which is terrible for everyone.

Part of dealing with our inability to listen means spending less distracted and manic time online – once we use the internet more markedly, we'll likely unlearn some of those twitchy behaviours that have carried over into our real-world lives – and another part is just practicing being better at it.

# ACTIVITY

How to listen in real life

---

* When someone is speaking to you, **try not to think.** Just listen. Repeat their words in your head if it helps.

* **Work on making eye contact or looking at something that isn't moving.** Fewer distractions mean you're more focused, and it also shows others that you're present.

* **Try to abandon the urge to respond as a reflex.** Instead, create a space for others to speak.

* **Ask questions.** Acknowledge what's been said and respond when there's space and quiet.

We're so used to ✳ DISTRACTIONS and BOREDOM and filling the silence and the space with pictures and videos and chats and noise, we're getting progressively worse at just sitting and hearing SOMEONE SPEAK

Chapter Eight

WHAT ELSE Is There?

While trying to change your relationship with the internet – arguably your biggest and most influential relationship – you'll likely feel like you're going through a kind of breakup. You might even have that pit-of-your-stomach feeling that you're pushing away the one thing in your life that's good and *gets you*, and a periodic paranoia that you've made a terrible mistake. You should've *never* detonated your life in this way! What harm would it *really* do if you were just to, say, text them right now and ask them to come over and never leave again?

Change won't be linear. It will happen in spurts and regressions. It will stop and start and feel good and bad. And it might help to have an on-hand reminder of all the things worth your time in life that have nothing at all to do with going or being online. Make your own list and see what's on it. Go after that stuff unshakeably.

Floating in the ocean. Or on a lake or in a pool. Finding money you forgot about. Eating a mango. Walking alone in the street with no music and no distractions. Listening to an album you haven't heard in a while. Going to a movie (and doing it alone). Meeting somebody new you like. Hearing somebody likes you. Having a pet sit on your lap, or your head, or your foot, or your anywhere. Dinner parties. Dinner out at a nice restaurant. Dinner out at an average restaurant. Dinner out. Dinner. A cup of coffee or tea. A clean fridge. A good sandwich. A good deal. Mandarins. Kiki's Delivery Service. Weeknight rain. Butter in a pan. Nice neighbours. Birthday presents. Mail that isn't bills. Saving up for something and then buying it and knowing you earned it. Biryani. Understanding something new. Getting hired. Being told you're looking well. Being told your hair looks healthy. Being told your smile is nice or your laugh is good or you're fun to be around. Smelling a scent you used to wear. Having your hair brushed. A beachside carnival, at night, in summer. ASMR videos of people massaging other people's heads. Getting paid! Shiny new sneakers. Dark bars for drinking lots. New underwear. Cinnamon donuts. Toast. Cows with curly hair. A good party and the texts the day after. Extremely crispy fried chicken. Dogs running on the beach.

Cereal for dinner. Thinking about yetis. And also Bigfoot. Also Nessie. Tiramisu. Coral. Reorganising your draws or cupboards. NBA half-time shows. Cherries. Hot chips. Big dark green mountains with fog around them. Fields of grass and the way the grass rolls in the wind. Fireworks. Lake Eildon. Most lakes. Underground train stations. Silver eyeshadow. Fields of sunflowers. The feet of your pets. The feet of other people's pets. Taking a good picture. A cold drink. A shawarma to line the stomach at 4 am. Running. Stretching. Laughing. When they're bringing your food to your table. Wearing a hat as a funky little accessory. Volcanos. A hard-boiled egg for breakfast. Sleeping. Sleeping in. When a domesticated animal pokes its head through a hole in a fence. Noodles in soup. Dumplings in soup. Pasta in soup. Weird lampshades and light fixtures. Wigs. Seeing a terrible person get their due. Poppies. Pickled ginger. A hot passport photo. Winning the card game, or the dice game, or any game. Beer. Autumn sun. New snow. Diners. Brown bear cubs. Sheep. Small goats. Stuffed peppers. Cake with your name on it. That time of night when it's not night yet but the sky is still lighter than the landscape and so it's like everything is a silhouette and then there's just sky colours. Snoopy. The Durutti Column. Panna cotta. Margaritas. 11 am.

Chapter Nine

GET ALL THE *Way Out,* JUST FOR A Minute

Your next task is to turn your devices off completely. Yes, completely. No, not forever. Just for little bits, sometimes, because it's important to try not being tethered to a tiny steel rectangle at least some of the time.

Choose a day where you won't need them to work, where you know you won't be stressed if you're AWOL. Stroke their little heads and tell them you're sorry and you did all you could and then turn them off. Don't worry, they won't feel a thing. In fact, they'll probably enjoy the peace and quiet; no fingers prodding at them, no turbulent trips down the street in a dark, deep shopper, no overheating or crashing of apps or freezing of windows. It'll be like a little vacation! For all of you.

Picture it: you're on one tropical island and your screens are on another. Like one of those weird couples' retreats. And you're passing the time on a banana lounge with the latest recommendation from Oprah's Book Club while the palm trees wriggle softly above you in the island breeze. You become a regular at the pool bar, where your fruity concoction is served to you in a hollowed-out melon with a cocktail umbrella in it, which is stuck into a slice of pineapple, and adorned by maraschino cherries. And your eyes, your brain, your fingers, and the nerves in your arms that have been working overtime since 2009, are absolutely loving it.

Meanwhile your phone is on island number two, flirting with a younger model.

While you don't know that, you do know that when you're all back together after this unchartered new chapter, you'll be better than ever. You'll appreciate each other more and see each other differently. You'll touch each other like it means something. But you'll also have a bit of yourselves back. And how good will it feel?

*Pretend that you have the STRENGTH to live in the world without the **CONSTANT, DEPENDABLE** noise of technology. Pretend it until it's true

People my age,
we've been
consuming media
since we were
five – it all seems
HYPER-FAMILIAR
to us and we're just
kind of BORED

Jaboukie Young-White

Once your phone and tablet and computer are off (sleep tight, my friends), you're going to want to put them somewhere out of sight, like in a drawer you don't use or away in a high-up cupboard. Maybe you want to give them to your housemate or parent or partner; someone who will happily guilt-trip you if you start sashaying around the topic of needing to 'look at something for a second'. Just remember to write a note on the fridge about where you've hidden them so you don't forget and have to look forever.

Take this alone time to do whatever you want. Pretend you're the last contestant in the *Big Brother* house and there are hours until your golf buggy comes to take you to the main stage for the finale. Or pretend it's 1871 and there's nothing else to do to pass the time except daisy chains and scrapbooks and wistfully looking out the window onto the farm.

If you must, pretend that you have the strength to live in the world without the constant, dependable noise of technology. Pretend until it's true.

Sing, cook, read, cut your fringe, clean under the bed, do 1000 push ups. Paint your nails, write a poem for a friend, think to yourself. Do whatever you want to do with that time, enjoy it, and try not to think about what you're missing. Because you're not missing anything you can't catch up on.

When you're ready to turn your devices on again, try exploring the internet and all the little corners like it's your first time. Find new people to follow, seek new communities, read until your eyes hurt. Get excited about all the new worlds to dive into and try doing it with a newfound finesse, as a seasoned professional with a fresh perspective. Ask your friends what their favourite internet worlds are, look into things you've been curious about. Watch YouTube videos called *First Time Hearing Dolly Parton Jolene REACTION* and *Great Depression Cooking – Depression Breakfast*. Try new browsers, new platforms, new modes, new communities. Try thinking of this as Phase Two.

# ACTIVITY

How to be slightly better at using the internet

If you're going to spend bits of time glued to your devices, and you will, you might as well make it a smoother ride. Here are some shortcuts that will make phone and computer use a little less time consuming.

* **Think of something you want to search while doing something else?** Take a note of it. Wait until you have five or more things you want to look into, then settle into a good old-fashioned session of googling stuff.

* **Hold down on the edge** of the iPhone's screen to show all windows.

* **Reopen a tab you've accidentally closed** by using Shift + Command + T on a Mac and Shift + Control + T on a PC.

* **Type 'docs.new' into your browser's address bar** to head straight to a fresh doc in Google Docs. Same for Google Sheets, Slides and Forms.

* **Pulling up the iPhone's control centre with the keyboard open can be sticky.** Swipe up as you usually would, but hold down until it appears.

* **Need to sign up to a website to view the content but don't want to get spammed?** Fakemailgenerator.com creates fake emails to protect you from unwanted comms.

* **You know that space bar pauses and plays a YouTube video** but did you know that pressing F takes you full screen, C brings up captions, M mutes the sound, and J rewinds ten seconds?

* **You can use emojis in your computer's browser** by pressing command, control, space bar on a Mac. For PCs, use Chrome, which has an emoji keyboard.

* **Install a grammar checker as an extension on Chrome** and it will check your work – and your emails and your texts and your posts – for grammar and tone.

* **You can quieten notifications with two taps.** Swipe right on an iPhone notification and tap 'Deliver quietly' or 'Turn off' for some peace and quiet!

* **Using your phone with one hand?** Getting cramps in your palm? Hold down the emoji or globe in your iPhone's keyboard and get either a right-stacked or left-stacked keyboard, so you're not straining to type.

* **If you don't already use Siri or Google Assistant or whatever helpful AI your device offers, try it.** Ask them to turn on your torch, set an alarm, tell you about the weather, calculate a sum. You'll do less picking up your phone and, as a result, less diving into the ether.

* **When your phone's AI mispronounces your name,** tell her 'that's not how you say my name'. She'll ask you how to say it and you'll never have to hear her butcher it again. Also, you might as well make her Irish while you're at it.

* **Stop apps and sites from asking you to review them** by going to your iPhone's settings and turning off 'In-App Ratings & Reviews' in the iTunes & Apps Stores tab.

* **You probably don't even know all the places you've logged in to Facebook before.** At your aunt's house, your ex's, your ex's aunt's. You can log out from all of them at once by going to your Facebook settings, then into Privacy and Security, and then into Where You're Logged In. Log me out, log me out, log me out. Feels like taking out the trash.

29 things to do instead of going online

* Build a mixtape for your crush or an imagined person
* Tidy your underwear drawer
* Learn a new recipe by heart
* Hand make some birthday cards
* Walk in a direction you haven't walked before
* Make a jug of iced tea for later
* Write a poem about the colour green
* Vacuum under your bed
* Go and sit in a cafe with a book
* Write down everything that happens for one week so you can read about it ten years from now
* Dye a tiny bit of your hair
* Pick a miniature bouquet of flowers from around the neighbourhood
* Write out your five best stories
* Buy some fabric and make tablecloths and napkins

* Make a list of everyone you've ever kissed
* Knit a giant, multi-coloured scarf
* Invent a cocktail or mocktail
* Start a new audiobook
* Sew a pair of shorts out of old material
* Rearrange a room
* Watch a movie classic you still haven't seen
* Send a letter to your oldest relative
* Go through old keepsakes and organise them by year
* Flip your mattress
* Listen to a friend or loved one's favourite album end-to-end
* Treat yourself to a massage
* Turn old or new trinkets into handmade keychains
* Reach out to a person you miss
* Burn some incense and lay on the floor

Conclusion

What's the point of getting offline in little bits, or curbing certain habits, or trying to work smarter, when we're likely going to be chained to some form of device forever and ever? (Unless the cabin in the woods thing works out ...).

It's about your brain. Your wellbeing and your health. Your relationships. Your text neck. It's about trying to ensure that – excuse the drama – when you're old and on your deathbed, you're not feeling a medley of devastated and resentful about all that time spent nose buried in screen. That you're not wishing you did more jumping and running and screaming and kissing, and less retweeting. More generally, it's about trying to make ourselves truly, properly happy. Not the kind of happy that comes from a meme (little, inside our head, a few messages back and forth in the DMs between friends), but the kind of happy that lives in us every day. The kind of happy that makes us better to be around, nicer to live with, more wonderful to know. The kind of happy you write home about.

You might not be there quite yet. I don't expect anything written in these pages has done something miraculous already, because even with the muting and deleting of the apps, you're still going to feel very tethered to your beautiful devices. That lovely, shiny little friend that you spent so long customising, teaching to know you, filling with things you care about. The thing that keeps you connected to Teresa in Guadalajara and Martin from that philosophy elective you took. The thing that keeps you plugged into the culture and totally-completely-always-abreast of the Happenings. That thing you adore because it, for some reason, always has videos of dogs doing stuff inside of it.

And, who knows, maybe you won't end up changing anything. Maybe you'll decide you actually love the mind-numbing stuff, that you don't want to change and you're sick of trying to be good, and everything was actually perfect before this book came along and messed it all up. Or ... maybe you'll find that you do change. That things feel a bit different, or more possible. Maybe you'll find that you don't really miss it like you thought you might, that it all becomes less shiny, less cool-to-the-touch, less of interest every day. That while you're still using it and occasionally loving it, you're not posting as much, so the likes aren't trickling in as often, and they've begun to lose some of their meaning. Maybe you'll find that lurking becomes more tedious, and mentions feel a bit like a burden. And that you're better off just dipping in now and then. If all goes to plan, you might find that the times you do engage feel fruitful and real, like sharing or gleaning important information, and staying up to date in the way you *thought* you were before. And that you're actually growing old, kind of. Getting more interested in birds and the sky at dusk and walking to work instead of catching that Uber you couldn't afford.

The hardest part will involve actually caving and resisting the urge to make a big deal out of it. It's fine, and bound to happen. You'll miss the timeline, the hours of meaningless fun. And they'll miss you. That's the hurtling freight train of life and there's not much you can do to stop it.

But no matter how much you stumble and splutter, you'll probably find the space between you and the internet widening, becoming more interesting, more full of potential. Maybe not so different to surfing after all.

Acknowledgment

I'd like to acknowledge the Traditional Custodians of the land on which I'm able to live and work, the Wurundjeri people of the Kulin Nation, whose culture is among the oldest living cultures in the world. I'd also like to extend my gratitude and respect to all Aboriginal and Torres Strait Islander people, and recognise the resilience and strength of your continuing cultures, and the monumental contributions made to our region, despite ongoing colonisation.

I believe in land rights, Treaty, and I recognise that sovereignty was never ceded.

If you are not Indigenous and, like me, live on stolen land, please join me in finding a way to make some kind of ongoing contribution to a relevant organisation as a form of paying the rent.

Further Reading

Quoted in this book:

* Donté Colley, dancer (@donte.colley)

* Ashley Feinberg, journalist (@ashelyfeinberg)

* Tavi Gevinson, writer and founder of *Rookie* (@tavitulle)

* Jenny Odell, author of *How To Do Nothing: Resisting the Attention Economy* (@the_jennitaur)

* Doreen St Félix, staff writer at The New Yorker (@dstfelix)

* Jia Tolentino, author of *Trick Mirror: Reflections on Self-Delusion* (@jiatolentino)

* Darcie Wilder, author of *Literally Show Me a Healthy Person* (@333333333433333)

* Jaboukie Young-White, writer and comedian (@jaboukie)

Publications:

* WIRED

* Quartz

* Vulture

* The Cut

* The Big Issue

* Jezebel

* The New Yorker

✳ **What's next? Why not count to 30 BEFORE picking up a screen?**

Published in 2021 by Hardie Grant Books, an imprint of Hardie Grant Publishing

Hardie Grant Books (Melbourne)
Building 1, 658 Church Street
Richmond, Victoria 3121

Hardie Grant Books (London)
5th & 6th Floors
52–54 Southwark Street
London SE1 1UN
hardiegrantbooks.com

Copyright text © Issy Beech 2021
Copyright design © Hardie Grant Publishing 2021

A catalogue record for this book is available from the National Library of Australia

How to Be Online and Also Be Happy
ISBN 9781743796610

10 9 8 7 6 5 4 3 2 1

Commissioning Editor: Alice Hardie-Grant
Editor: Libby Turner
Design Manager: Mietta Yans
Designer: Ngaio Parr
Production Manager: Todd Rechner

Colour reproduction by Splitting Image Colour Studio
Printed in China by Leo Paper Products LTD.

The paper this book is printed on is from certified FSC® certified forests and other sources. FSC® promotes environmentally responsible, socially beneficial and economically viable management of the world's forests.

Hardie Grant acknowledges the Traditional Owners of the country on which we work, the Wurundjeri people of the Kulin nation and the Gadigal people of the Eora nation, and recognises their continuing connection to the land, waters and culture. We pay our respects to their Elders past, present and emerging.

Survive the Modern World

Upskill and expand your knowledge with these accessible pocket guides.

Available now

Survive the Modern World

How to **THINK** like an **ACTIVIST**

Wendy Syfret

Survive the Modern World

How *to start* A SIDE Hustle

Kaylene Langford

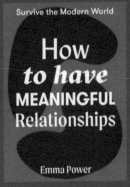

Survive the Modern World

How *to have* MEANINGFUL Relationships

Emma Power